CONTENTS

T0087264

ALWAYS ON MY MIND

Words and Music by WAYNE THOMPSON,
MARK JAMES and JOHNNY CHRISTOPHER

Moderately slow

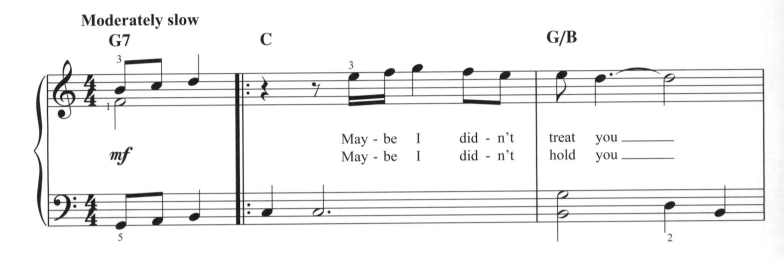

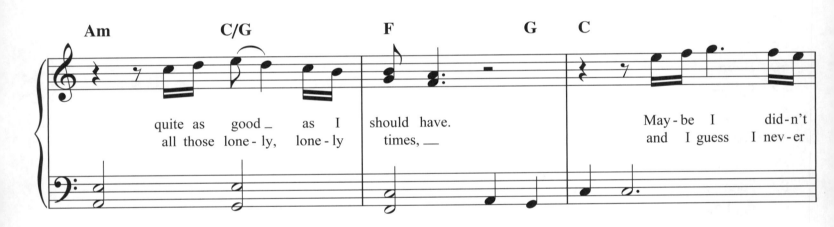

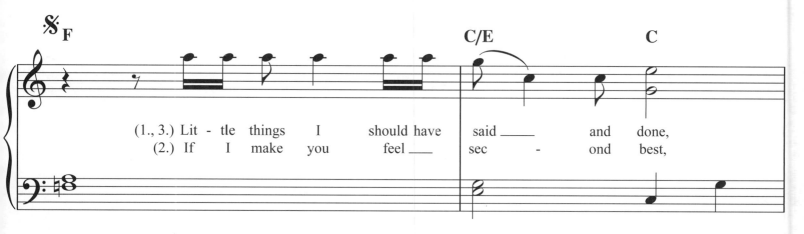

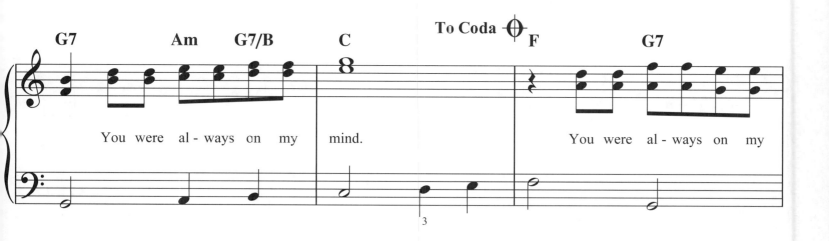

6

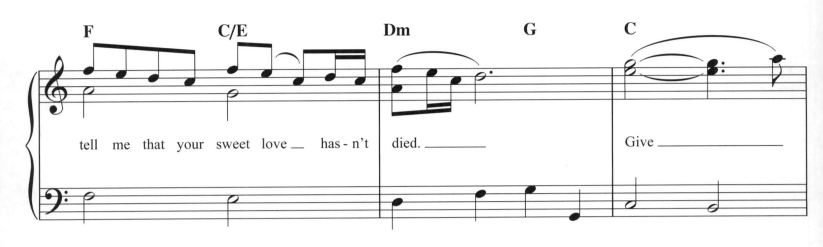

tell me that your sweet love __ has-n't died. _____ Give _____

me, _____ give me one more chance to keep you sat - is - fied, _____ ____ sat - is -

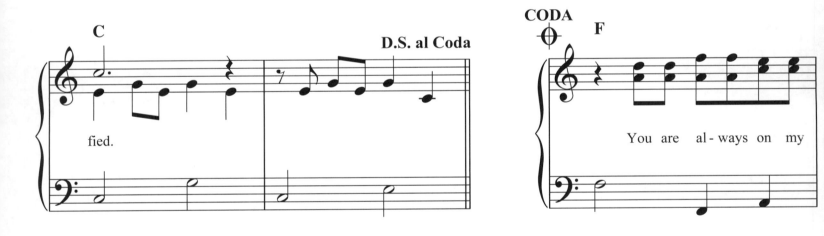

fied. _____ You are al - ways on my

mind. _____ ____ You are al-ways on my mind. *rall.*

BLUE

Words and Music by
BILL MACK

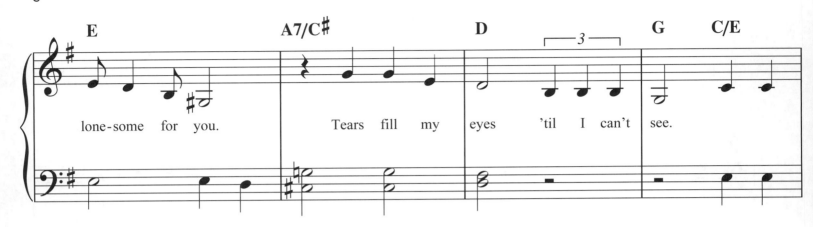

lone-some for you.　　Tears fill my eyes　'til I can't see.

(Solo ends)

Three o' clock in the morn - ing,
Now that it's o - ver,

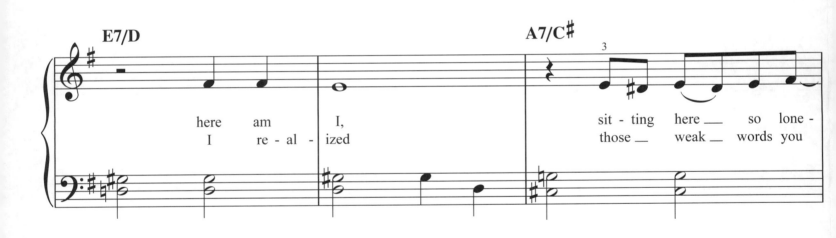

here am I,
I re - al - ized

sit - ting here ___ so lone -
those ___ weak ___ words you

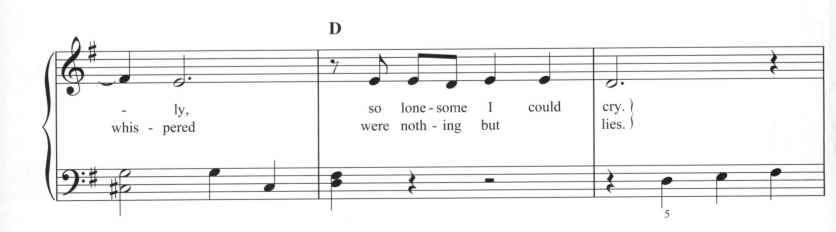

- ly,
whis - pered

so lone - some I could cry.
were noth - ing but lies.

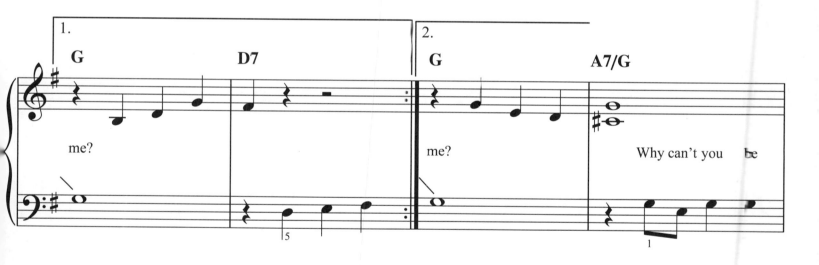

AMAZED

Words and Music by MARV GREEN,
CHRIS LINDSEY and AIMEE MAYO

Moderately slow

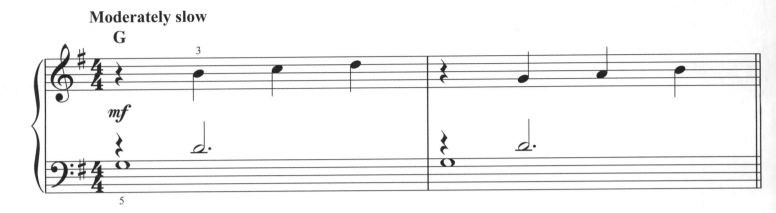

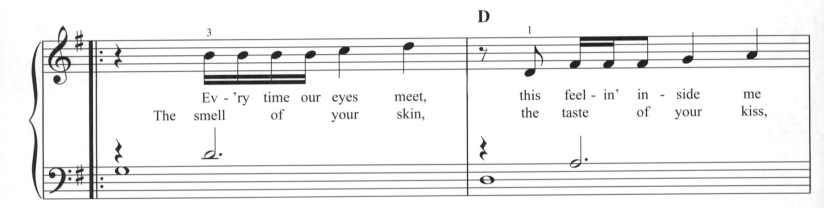

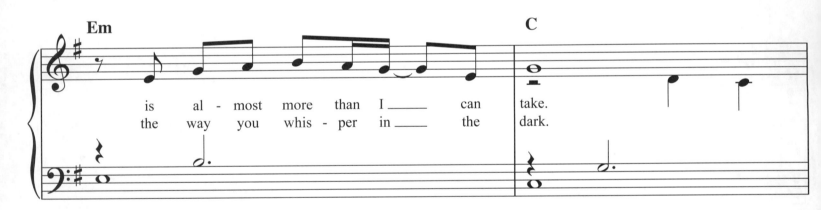

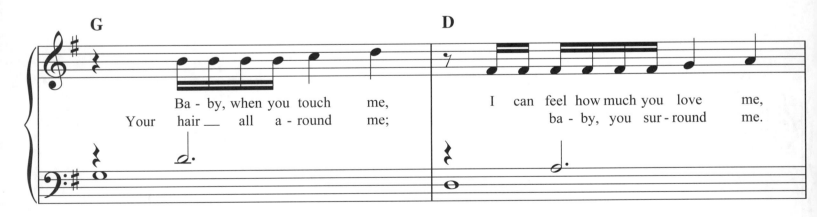

for - ev - er and ev - er. _____ Ev-'ry lit - tle thing that you do, _

_____ ba - by, I'm a - mazed _ by you. _

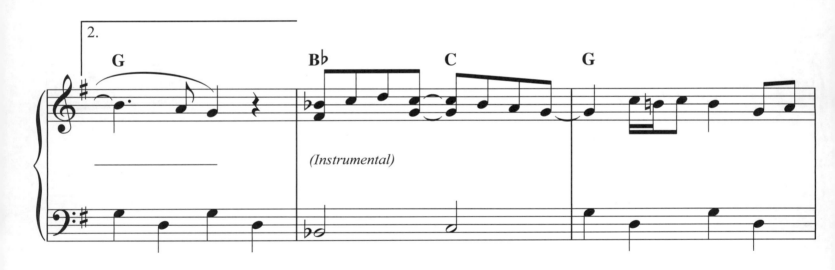

_____ (Instrumental)

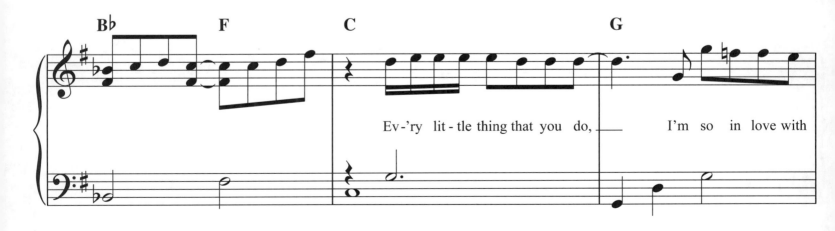

Ev-'ry lit - tle thing that you do, ____ I'm so in love with

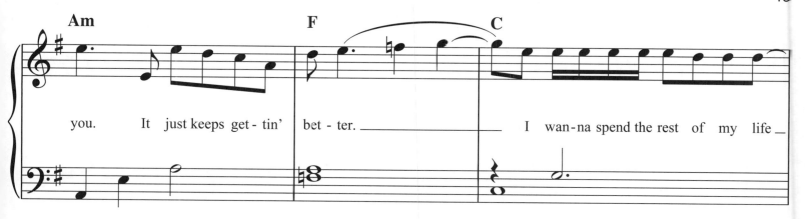

you.   It   just keeps get - tin'   bet - ter. _____   I   wan-na spend the rest   of   my   life ___

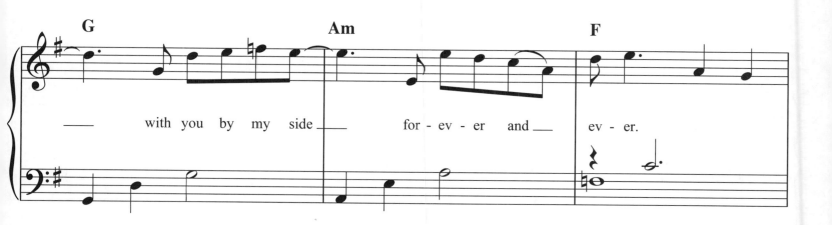

___   with you by my side ___   for - ev - er   and ___   ev - er.

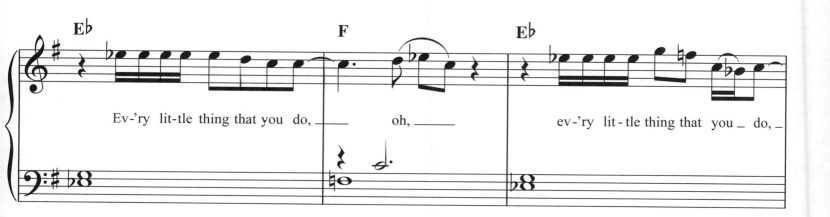

Ev-'ry lit-tle thing that you do, ___   oh, ___   ev-'ry lit-tle thing that you _ do, _

___   ba- by, I'm a - mazed _ by ___   you.

BLUE BAYOU

Words and Music by ROY ORBISON
and JOE MELSON

Moderately

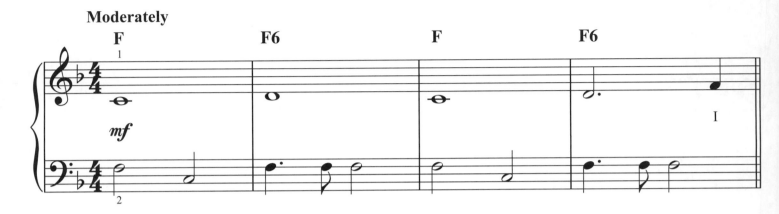

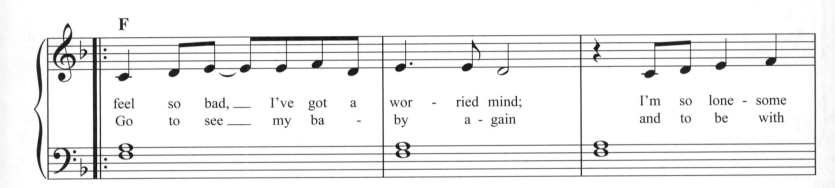

feel so bad, __ I've got a wor - ried mind;
Go to see __ my ba - by a - gain

I'm so lone - some
and to be with

all the time,
some of my friends;

since I left my
may - be I'd be

ba - by be - hind __ on __
hap - py then __ on __

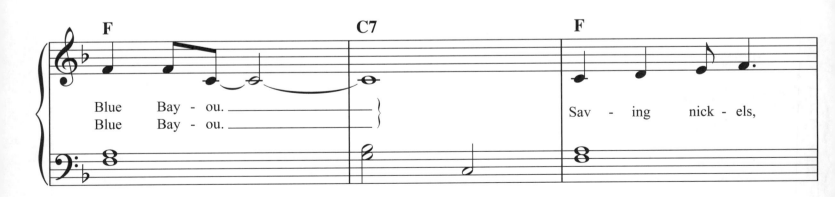

Blue Bay - ou. ___
Blue Bay - ou. ___

Sav - ing nick - els,

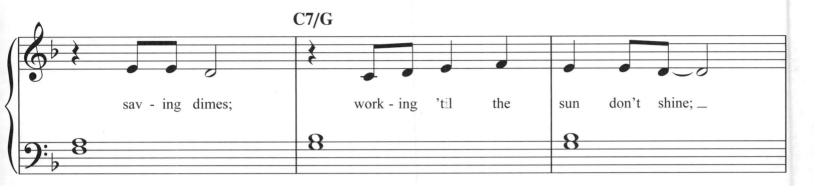

C7/G

sav - ing dimes; work - ing 'til the sun don't shine; —

F

look - ing for - ward to hap - pi - er times — on Blue Bay - ou. —

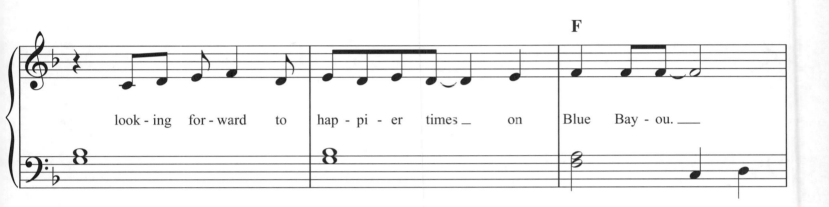

E♭   **F**

I'm go - ing back some day, — come what may — to
I'm go - ing back some day, — gon - na stay — on

C7

Blue Bay - ou, _____ where you sleep all day — and the
Blue Bay - ou, _____ where the folks are fine — and the

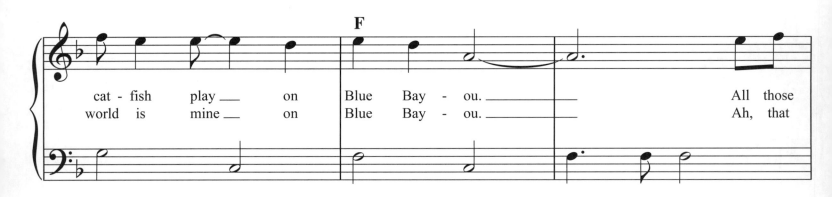

cat - fish play ___ on Blue Bay - ou. ___ All those
world is mine ___ on Blue Bay - ou. ___ Ah, that

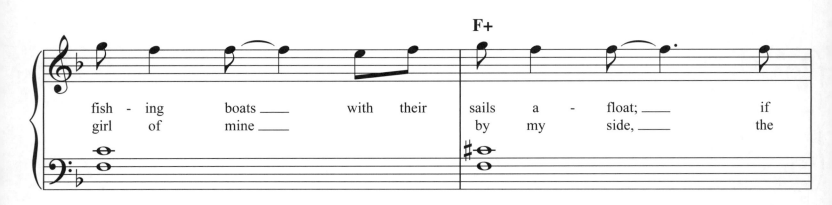

fish - ing boats ___ with their sails a - float; ___ if
girl of mine ___ by my side, ___ the

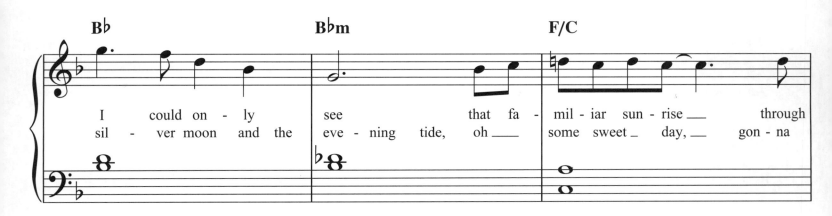

I could on - ly see that fa - mil - iar sun - rise ___ through
sil - ver moon and the eve - ning tide, oh ___ some sweet __ day, __ gon - na

1.

sleep - y eyes, __ how hap - py I'd be. ___
take a - way __ this

BUSTED

Words and Music by
HARLAN HOWARD

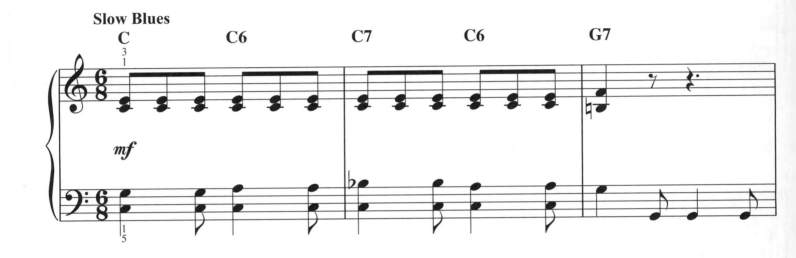

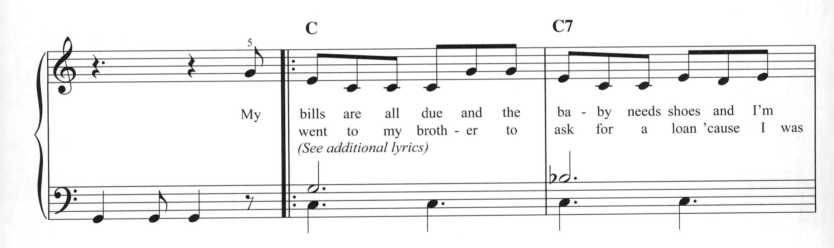

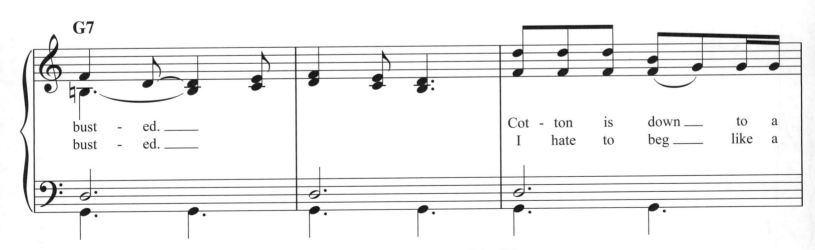

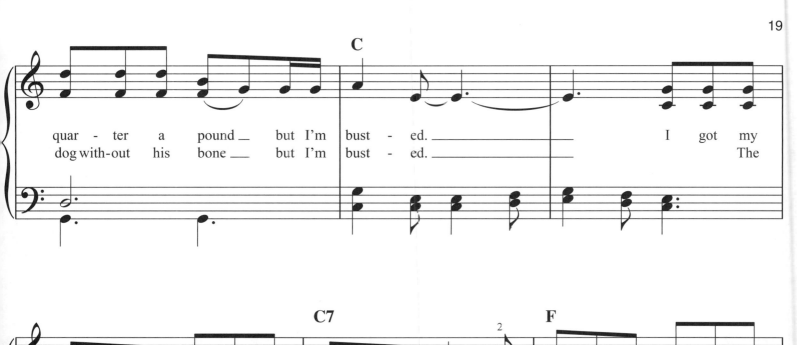

quar - ter a pound ___ but I'm bust - ed. _____ I got my
dog with-out his bone ___ but I'm bust - ed. _____ The

cow that went dry and a hen that won't lay, a big stack of bills that gets
broth - er said, "There ain't a thing I can do; my wife and my kids are all

big - ger each day. The coun - ty's gon - na haul my be - long - ings a - way 'cause I'm
down with the flu; and I was just think-ing a - bout call - ing on you! And I'm

1., 2.

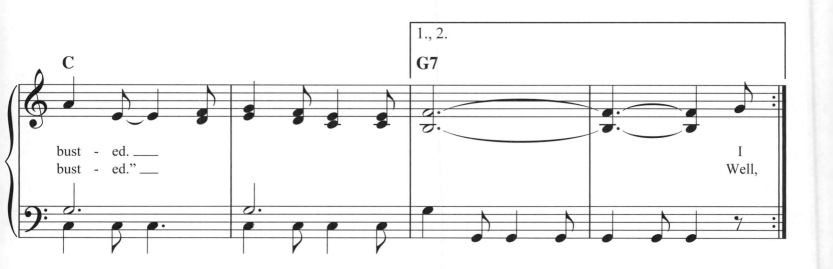

bust - ed. ___
bust - ed." ___ Well,
I

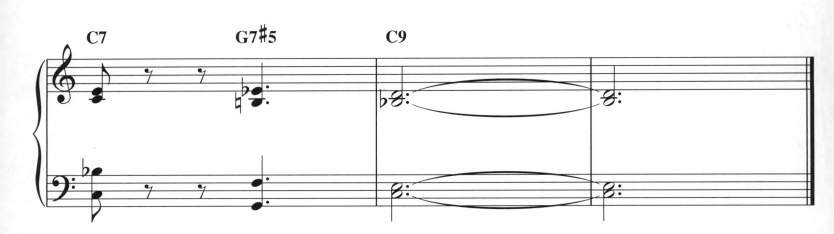

Additional Lyrics

Well, I am no thief but a man can go wrong when he's busted.
The food that we canned last summer is gone and I'm busted.
The fields are all bare and the cotton won't grow.
Me and my fam'ly got to pack up and go,
But I'll make a living, just where I don't know 'cause I'm busted.

BLUE EYES CRYING IN THE RAIN

Words and Music by
FRED ROSE

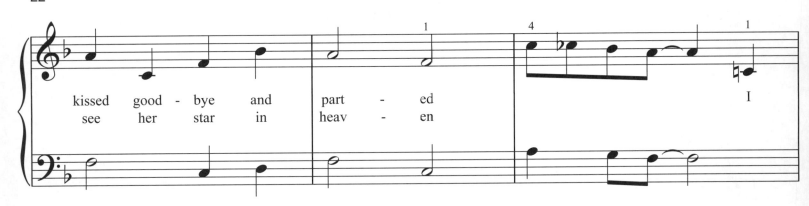

kissed good - bye and part - ed
see her star in heav - en

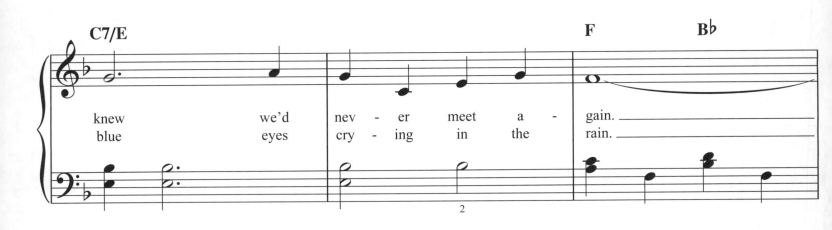

C7/E   **F**   **B♭**

knew we'd nev - er meet a - gain. _____
blue eyes cry - ing in the rain. _____

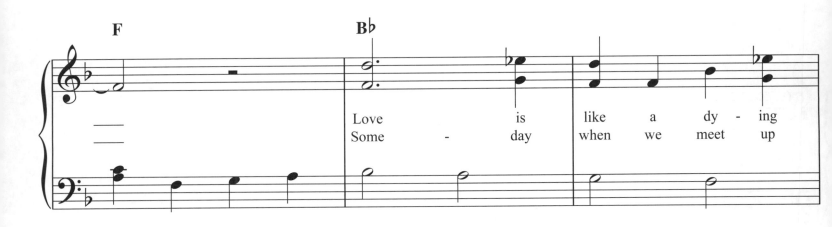

F   **B♭**

_____ Love is like a dy - ing
Some - day when we meet up

F

em - ber _____
yon - der _____ on - ly
we'll stroll

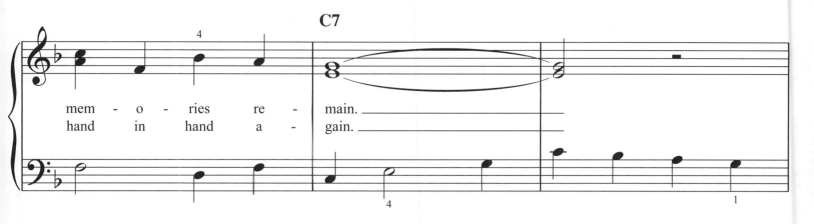

C7

mem - o - ries re - main. _____
hand in hand a - gain. _____

F

Through the ag - es I'll re - mem - ber
In a land that knows no part - ing

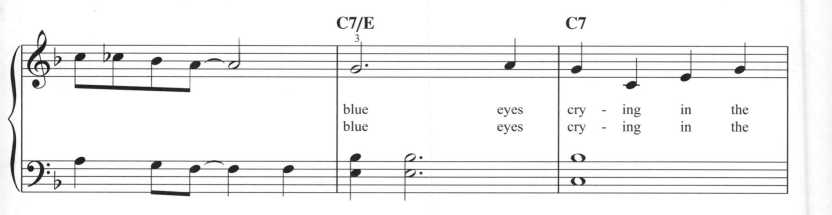

C7/E   **C7**

blue eyes cry - ing in the
blue eyes cry - ing in the

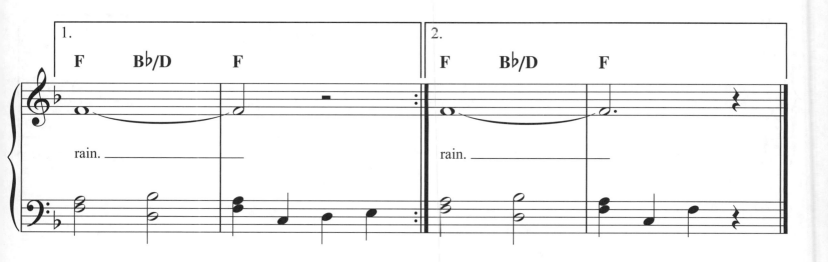

1.
F   **B♭/D**   **F**

rain. _____

2.
F   **B♭/D**   **F**

rain. _____

BOOT SCOOTIN' BOOGIE

Words and Music by
RONNIE DUNN

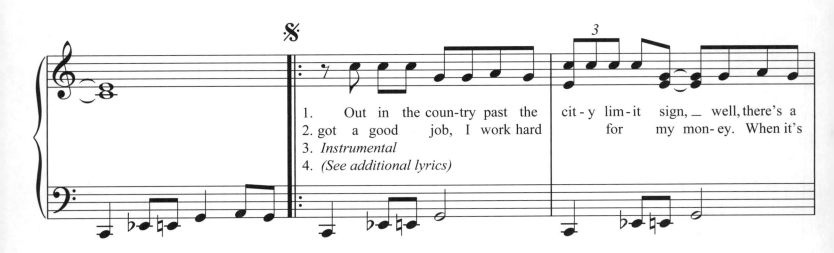

1. Out in the coun-try past the cit-y lim-it sign, __ well, there's a
2. got a good job, I work hard for my mon-ey. When it's
3. *Instrumental*
4. *(See additional lyrics)*

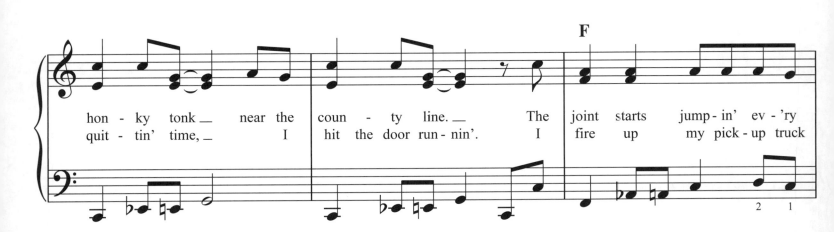

hon-ky tonk __ near the coun-ty line. __ The joint starts jump-in' ev-'ry
quit-tin' time, __ I hit the door run-nin'. I fire up my pick-up truck

boot scoot - in'! _____ Whoa, Cad - il - lac, Black - jack,

ba - by, meet me out back, we're gon - na boo - gie. _____ Oh,

get down, turn a - round, go to town, boot scoot - in' boo - gie. _____

1.

2. D.S.

Whoa.

3.

I said

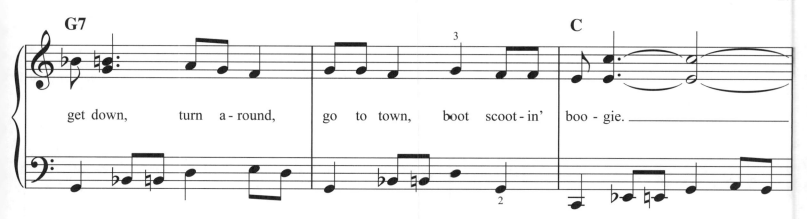

get down, turn a - round, go to town, boot scoot-in' boo - gie.

Whoa, get down, turn a - round, go to town, boot scoot- in'

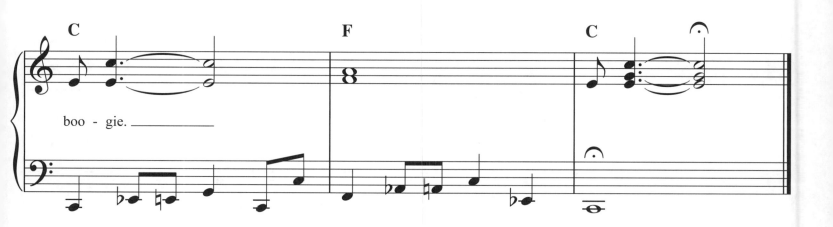

boo - gie.

Additional Lyrics

4. The bartender asks me, says,
   "Son, what will it be?"
   I want a shot at that redhead yonder lookin' at me.
   The dance floor's hoppin'
   And it's hotter than the Fourth of July.
   I see outlaws, inlaws, crooks and straights
   All out makin' it shake doin' the boot scootin' boogie.
   Chorus

BY THE TIME I GET TO PHOENIX

Words and Music by
JIMMY WEBB

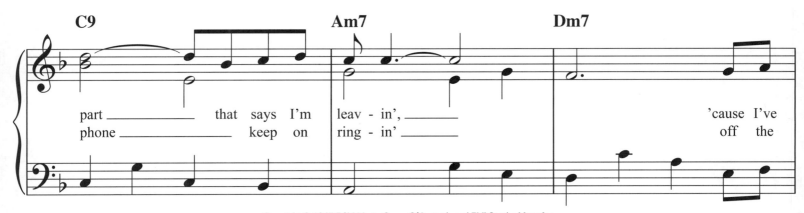

left that girl ____ so man-y times ____ be - fore. ____ By the

wall, that's all. ____ By the

time I make O - kla - ho - ma ____ she'll be sleep - in'; ____

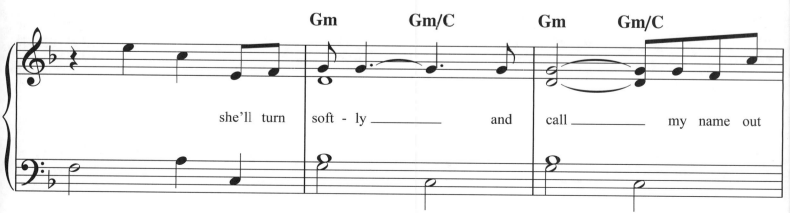

she'll turn soft - ly ____ and call ____ my name out

Fmaj7 ... **B♭maj7**

low. And she'll cry just to

C9 ... **Am7** ... **Dm7**

think _____ I'd real - ly leave her, _____ though _

Gm7 ... **C7** ... **Fmaj7**

time and time _____ I've tried _ to tell her so;

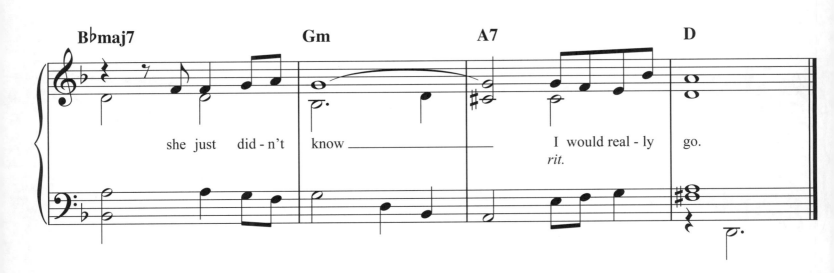

B♭maj7 ... **Gm** ... **A7** ... **D**

she just did - n't know _____ I would real - ly go.

rit.

COULD I HAVE THIS DANCE

from URBAN COWBOY

Words and Music by WAYLAND HOLYFIELD
and BOB HOUSE

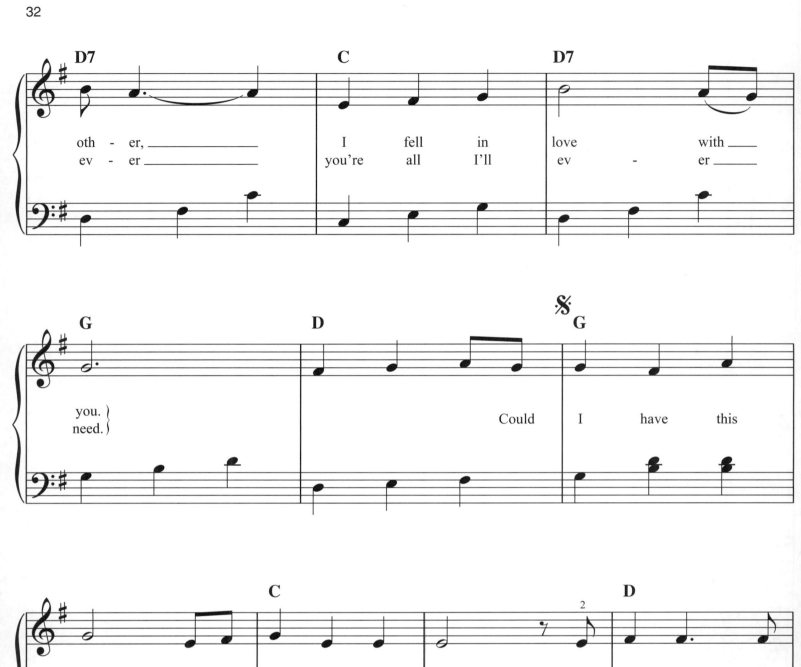

8vb

CHATTAHOOCHEE

Words and Music by JIM McBRIDE
and ALAN JACKSON

Bright Country 2-step

Way down yon-der on the Chat - ta - hoo - chee
fogged up the win-dows in _____ my old Chev - y;

it gets hot - ter than a hoo - chie coo - chie.
I was will - in' but _____ she was - n't read - y. So, I

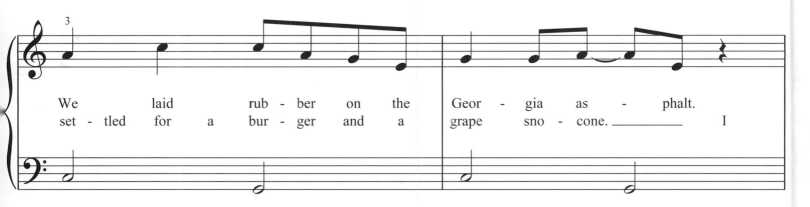

We laid rub - ber on the Geor - gia as - phalt.
set - tled for a bur - ger and a grape sno - cone. _____ I

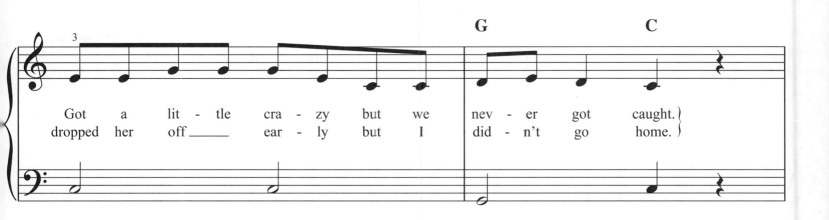

Got a lit - tle cra - zy but we nev - er got caught.
dropped her off _____ ear - ly but I did - n't go home.

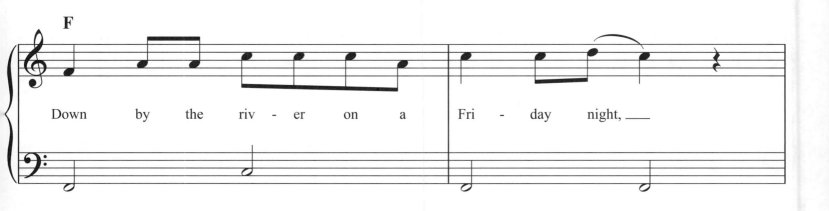

Down by the riv - er on a Fri - day night, ___

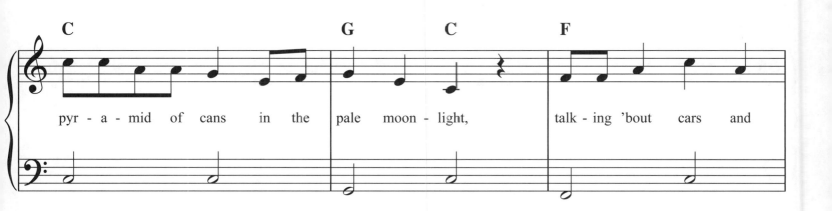

pyr - a - mid of cans in the pale moon - light, talk - ing 'bout cars and

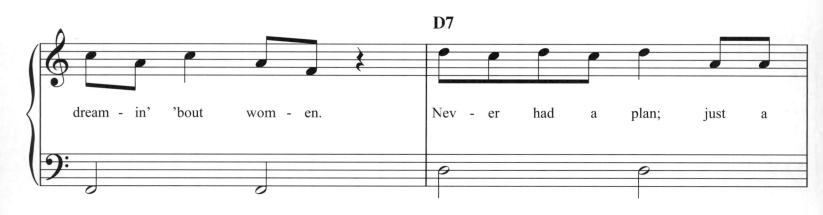

dream - in' 'bout wom - en. Nev - er had a plan; just a

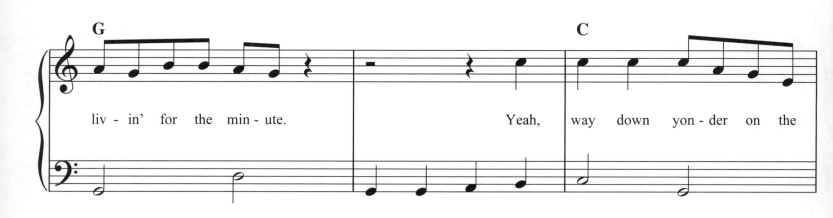

liv - in' for the min - ute. Yeah, way down yon - der on the

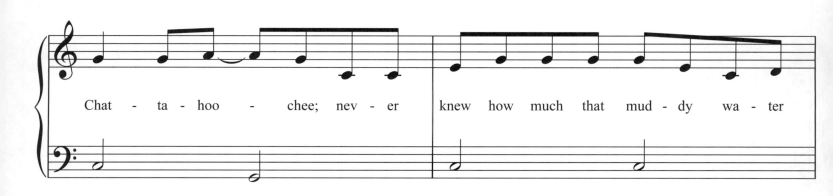

Chat - ta - hoo - chee; nev - er knew how much that mud - dy wa - ter

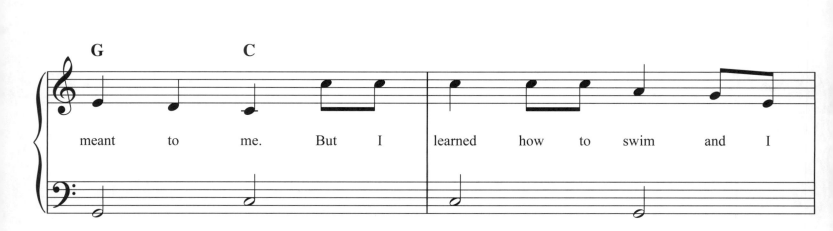

meant to me. But I learned how to swim and I

37

learned who I was; a lot a - bout liv - in' and a lit - tle 'bout love.

Well, we

lit - tle 'bout love, a lot a - bout liv - in' and a lit - tle 'bout __ love.

rit.

CRAZY

Words and Music by
WILLIE NELSON

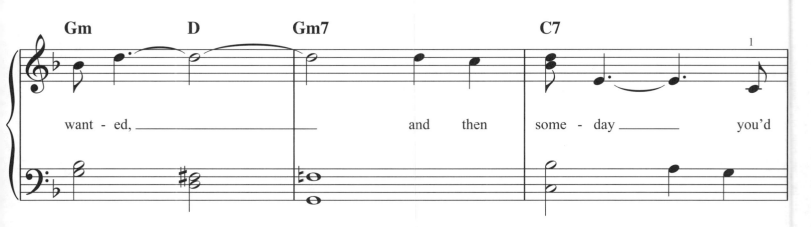

want - ed, _____ and then some - day _____ you'd

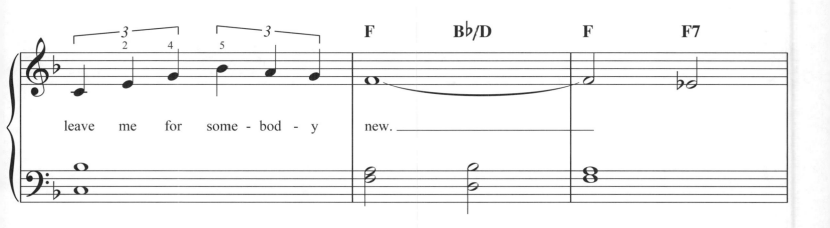

leave me for some - bod - y new. _____

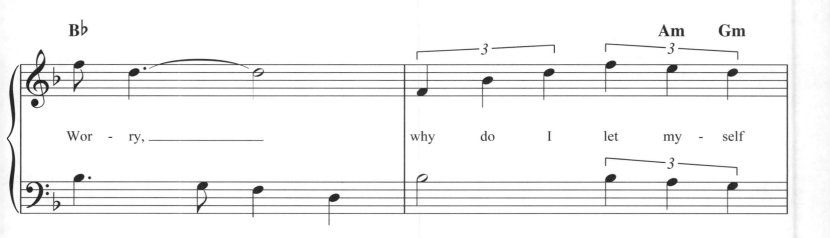

Wor - ry, _____ why do I let my - self

wor - ry, _____ won - d'rin' _____

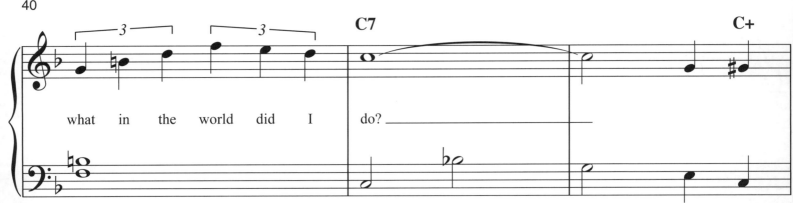

C7 **C+**

what in the world did I do? _____

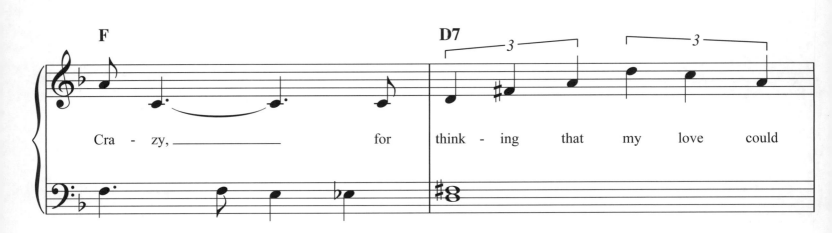

F **D7**

Cra - zy, _____ for think - ing that my love could

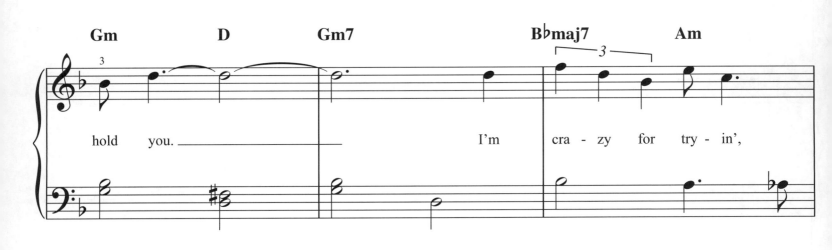

Gm **D** **Gm7** **B♭maj7** **Am**

hold you. _____ I'm cra - zy for try - in',

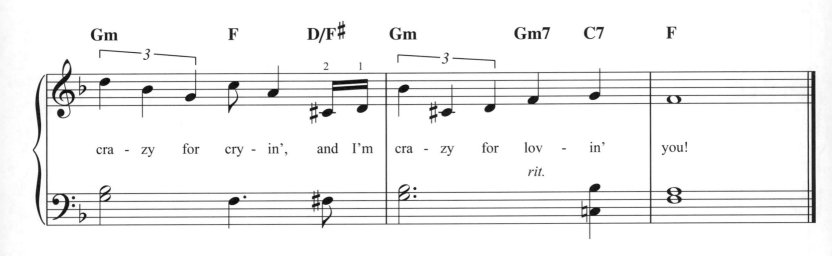

Gm **F** **D/F♯** **Gm** **Gm7** **C7** **F**

cra - zy for cry - in', and I'm cra - zy for lov - in' you!

rit.

CRYIN' IN THE CHAPEL

Words and Music by
ARTIE GLENN

Slowly, with expression

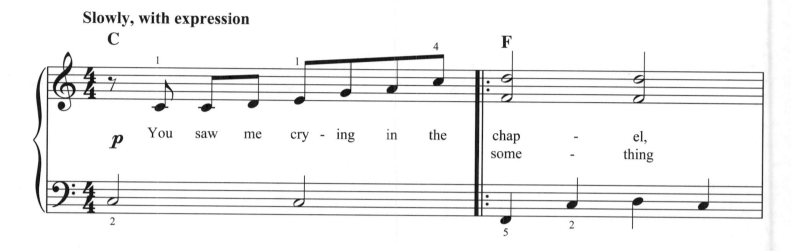

You saw me cry - ing in the chap - el,
some - thing

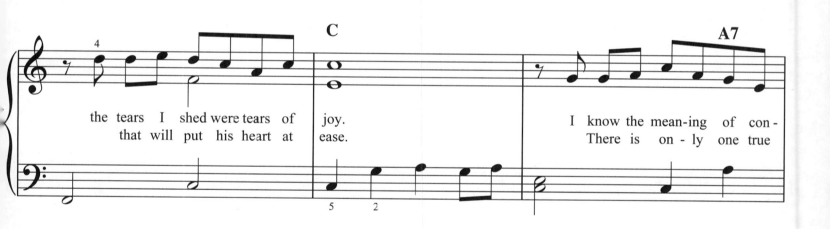

the tears I shed were tears of joy.
that will put his heart at ease.
I know the mean-ing of con -
There is on - ly one true

tent - ment,
an - swer,
now I am hap - py with the Lord.
he must get down on his knees.

Just a plain and sim - ple chap - el,
Meet your neigh-bor in the chap - el,

where hum - ble peo - ple go to
join with him in tears of

pray:
joy.

I pray the Lord that I'll grow strong - er,
You'll know the mean - ing of con - tent - ment,

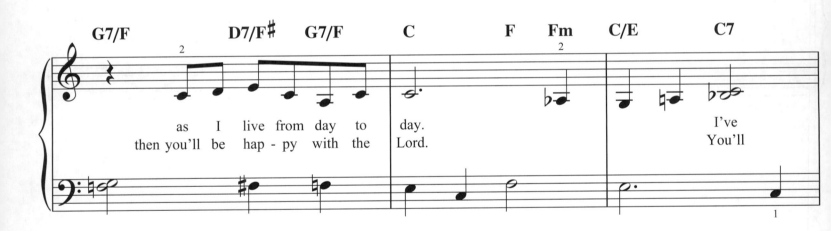

as I live from day to day.
then you'll be hap - py with the Lord.

I've
You'll

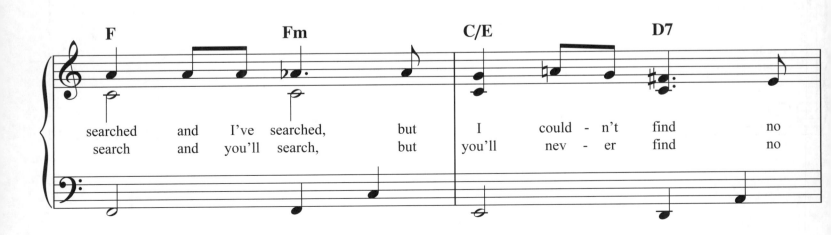

searched and I've searched, but I could - n't find no
search and you'll search, but you'll nev - er find no

CRYING

Words and Music by ROY ORBISON
and JOE MELSON

I was all right for a while I could
I was o - ver you but it's

smile for a - while. But I saw you last night, you held my
true, so true I love you e - ven more than I

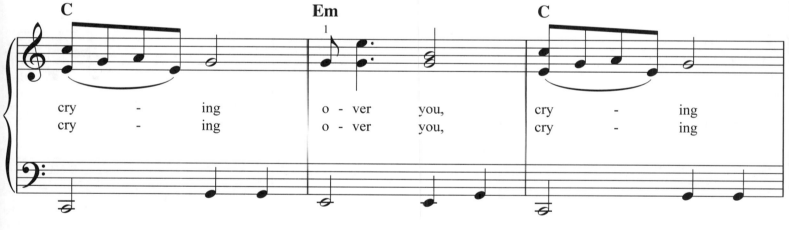

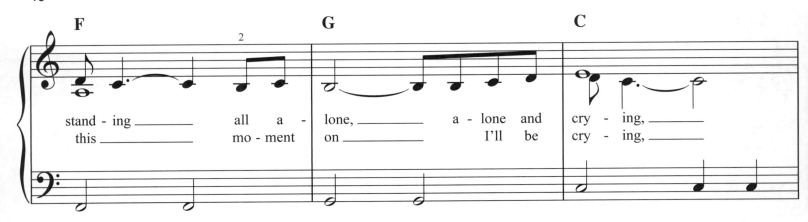

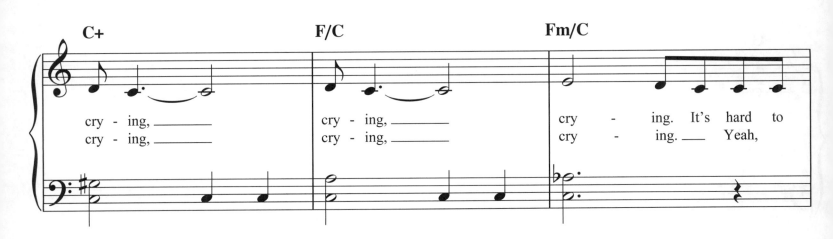

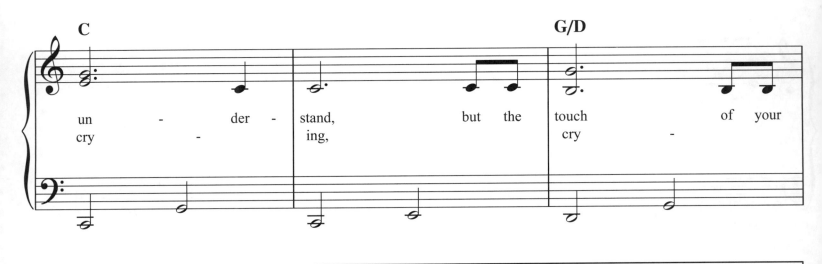

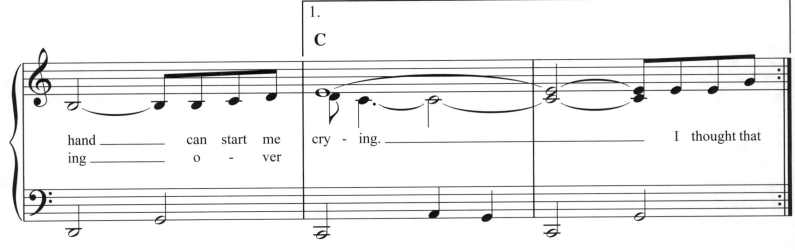

DADDY SANG BASS

Words and Music by
CARL PERKINS

Moderate Country 2 beat

mf

I re-mem-ber when I was a lad, times were hard and things were bad. But there's a sil-ver lin-ing be-hind ev-'ry cloud. _____ Just poor peo-ple, that's what we

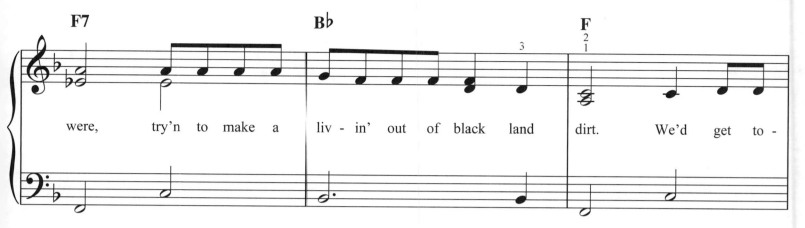

were, try'n to make a liv - in' out of black land dirt. We'd get to-

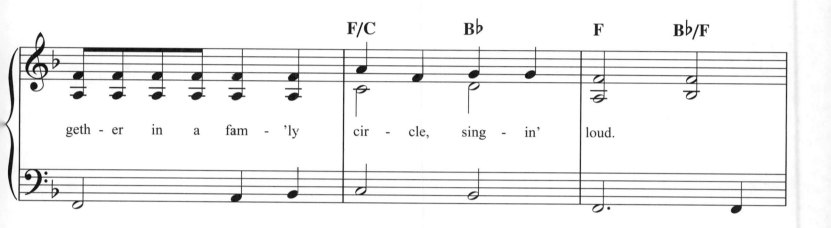

geth - er in a fam - 'ly cir - cle, sing - in' loud.

Dad - dy sang bass, Ma - ma sang ten - or. Me and lit - tle

broth - er would join right in there. Sing - in' seems to

Dm   **G**   **C**

help a trou - bled soul.   One of these

F   **F7**   **Bb**

days and it won't be long, I'll re - join them in a

F   **C7**

song. I'm gon - na join the fam - 'ly cir - cle at the

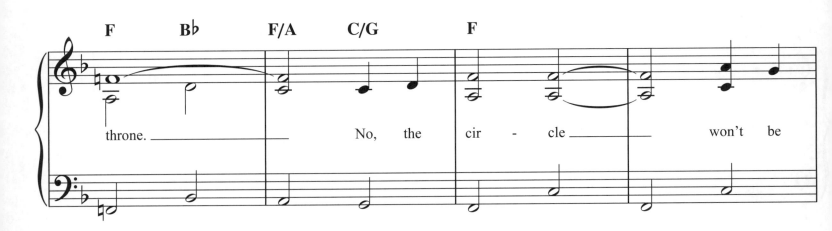

F   **Bb**   **F/A**   **C/G**   **F**

throne. _____ No, the cir - cle _____ won't be

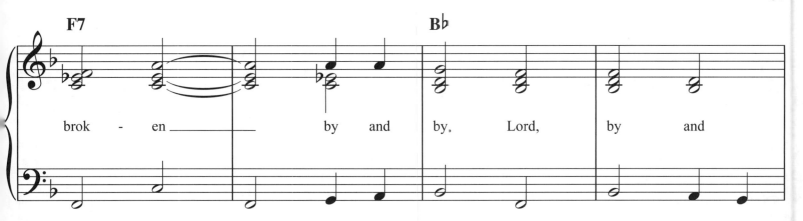

brok - en _____ by and by, Lord, by and

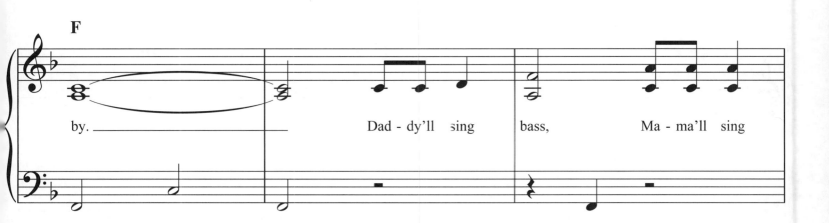

by. _____ Dad - dy'll sing bass, Ma - ma'll sing

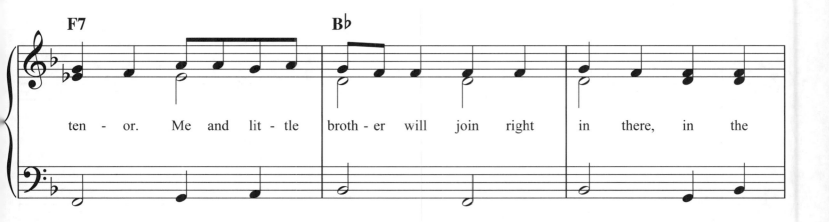

ten - or. Me and lit - tle broth - er will join right in there, in the

sky, Lord, _____ in the sky. _____ I re -

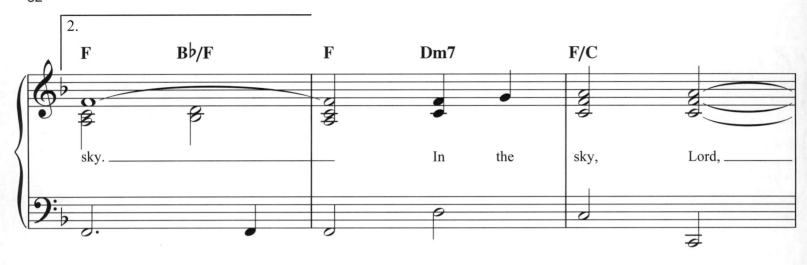

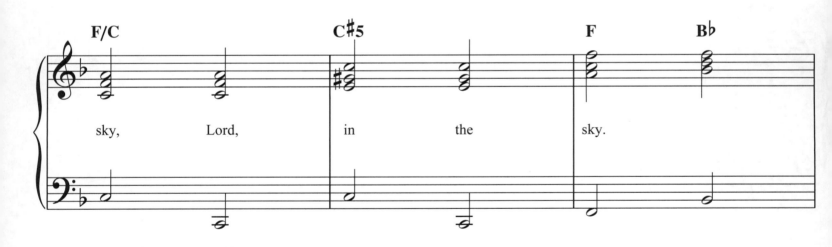

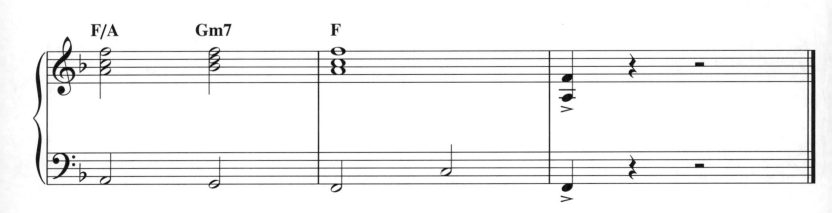

DON'T IT MAKE MY BROWN EYES BLUE

Words and Music by
RICHARD LEIGH

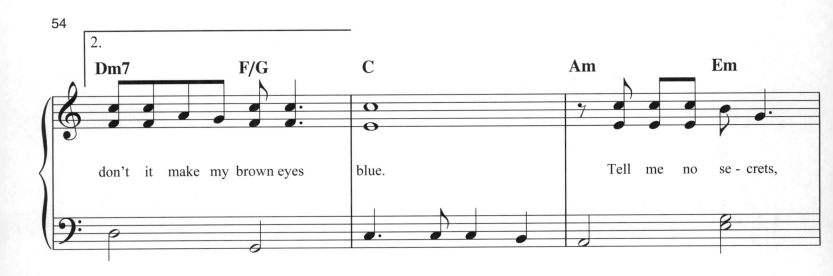

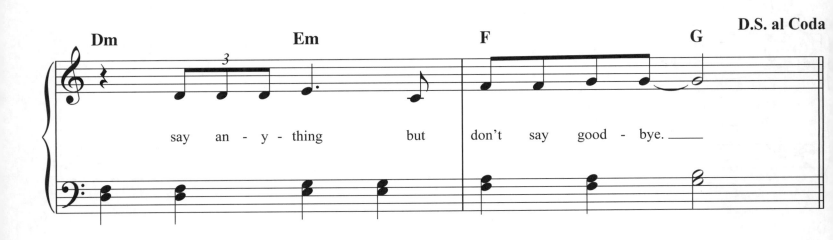

CODA

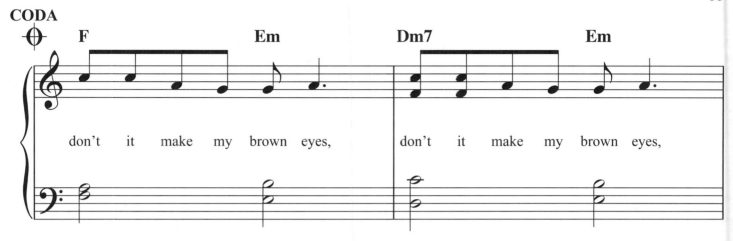

don't it make my brown eyes, don't it make my brown eyes,

don't it make my brown eyes...

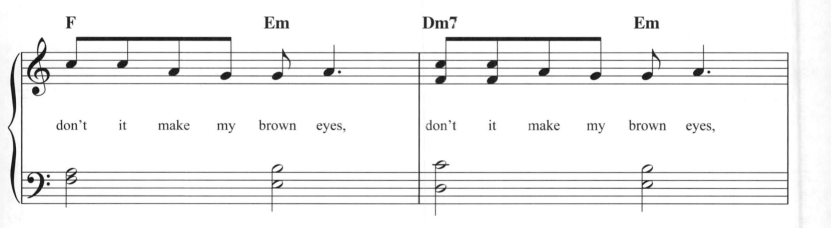

don't it make my brown eyes, don't it make my brown eyes,

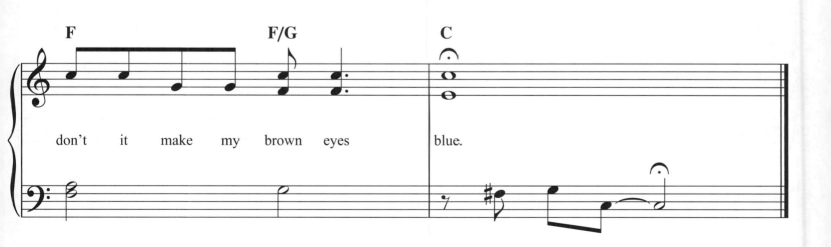

don't it make my brown eyes blue.

DREAM BABY
(How Long Must I Dream)

Words and Music by
CINDY WALKER

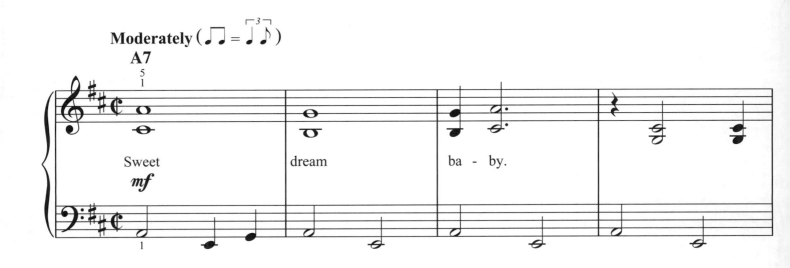

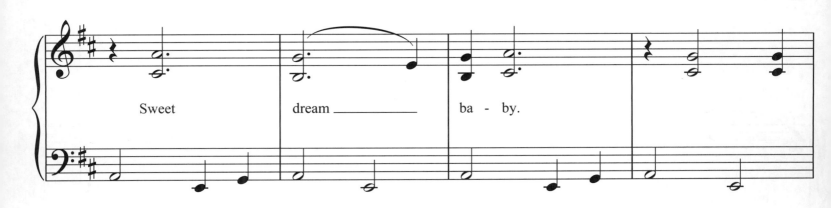

and I'm dream-in' of you. That won't do. _____

Dream ba - by, make me stop my dream-in'. You can make my dreams _ come

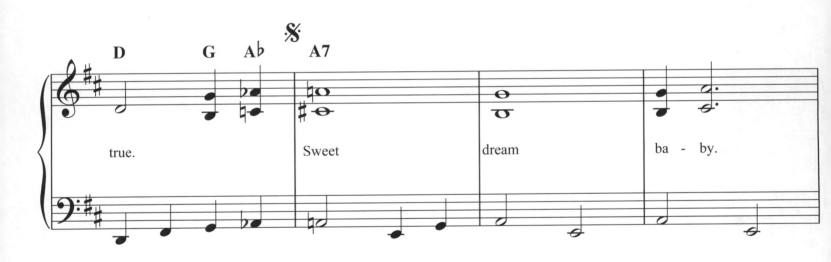

true. Sweet dream ba - by.

Sweet dream _____ ba - by.

ELVIRA

Words and Music by
DALLAS FRAZIER

Moderately

El - vi - ra,   El - vi - ra,

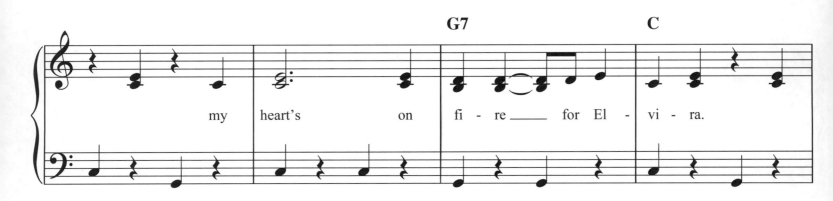

my   heart's   on   fi - re _____ for El - vi - ra.

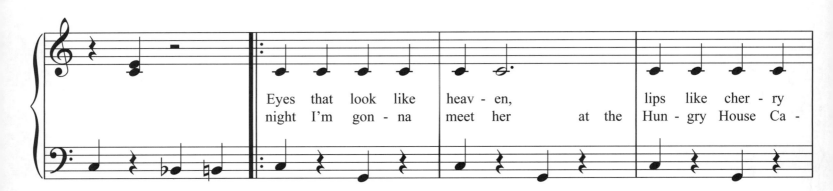

Eyes that look like   heav - en,   lips like cher - ry
night I'm gon - na   meet her   at the   Hun - gry House Ca -

wine, that girl can sho' nuff make my lit - tle light shine. _____
fe. And I'm gon-na give her all the love __ I can. _____

_____ I get a fun - ny feel - ing up and down my
_____ She's gon-na jump and hol - ler 'cause I saved up my last two

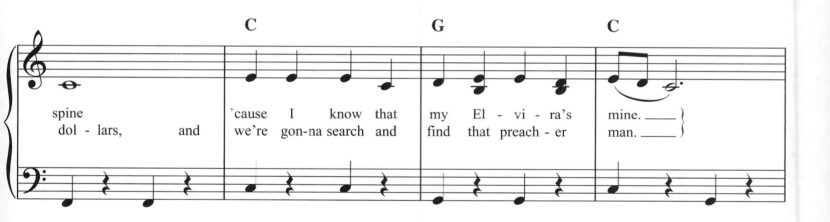

spine 'cause I know that my El - vi - ra's mine. ____ }
dol - lars, and we're gon-na search and find that preach - er man. ____ }

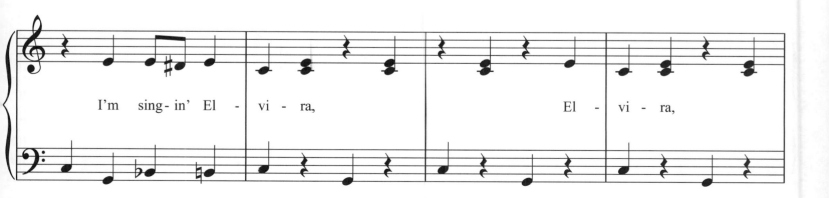

I'm sing-in' El - vi - ra, El - vi - ra,

my heart's on fi - re _____ for El - vi - ra.

Gid - dy - up, a oom pa - pa oom pa - pa mow mow,

gid - dy - up, a oom pa - pa oom pa - pa mow mow, hi - yo Sil - ver a -

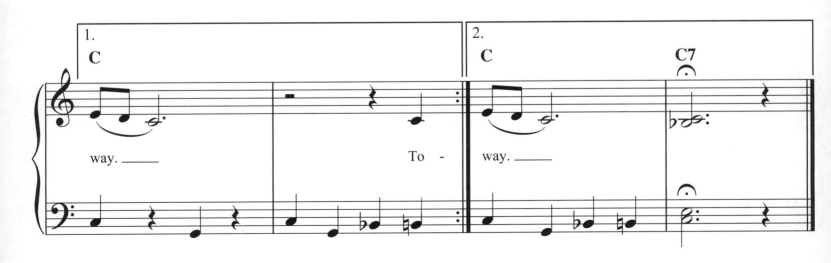

way. _____   To -   way. _____

EL PASO

Words and Music by
MARTY ROBBINS

Moderately

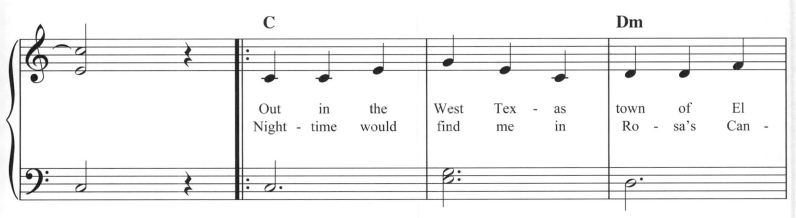

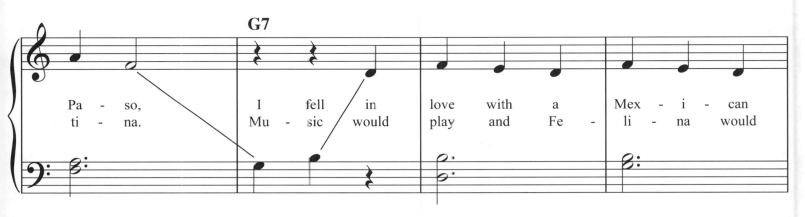

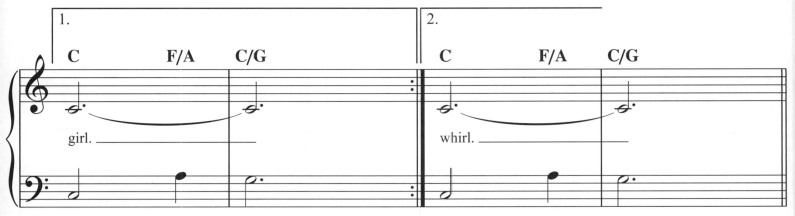

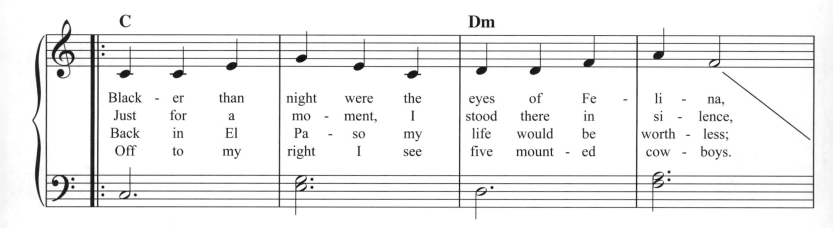

C **Dm**

Black - er than | night were the | eyes of Fe - li - na,
Just for a | mo - ment, I | stood there in | si - lence,
Back in El | Pa - so my | life would be | worth - less;
Off to my | right I see | five mount - ed | cow - boys.

G7 **C** **F/A**

wick - ed | and | e - vil while | cast - ing a | spell. ____
shocked by | the | foul e - vil | deed I had | done. ____
ev - 'ry - | thing's | gone, in life | noth - ing is | left. ____
Off to | my | left ride a | doz - en or | more. ____

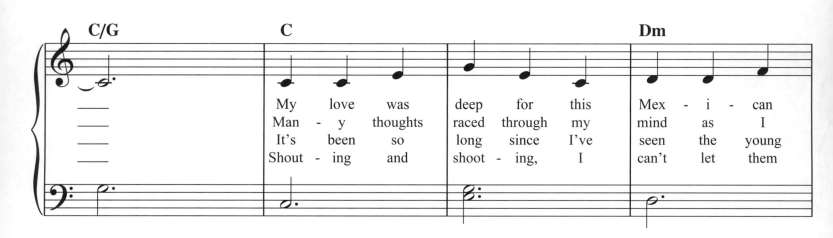

C/G **C** **Dm**

____ | My love was | deep for this | Mex - i - can
____ | Man - y thoughts | raced through my | mind as I
____ | It's been so | long since I've | seen the young
____ | Shout - ing and | shoot - ing, I | can't let them

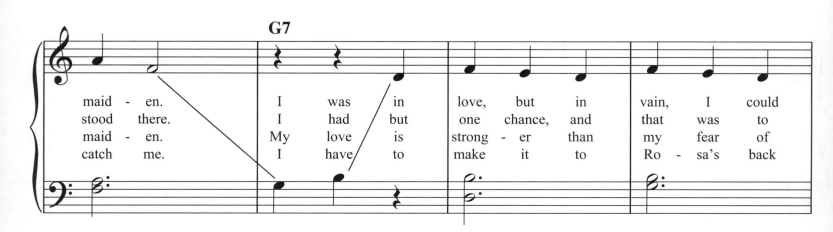

G7

maid - en. | I was in | love, but in | vain, I could
stood there. | I had but | one chance, and | that was to
maid - en. | My love is | strong - er than | my fear of
catch me. | I have to | make it to | Ro - sa's back

65

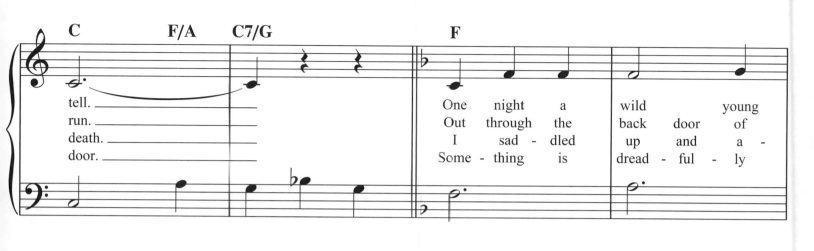

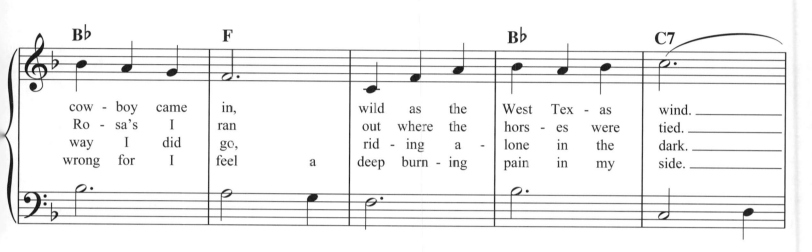

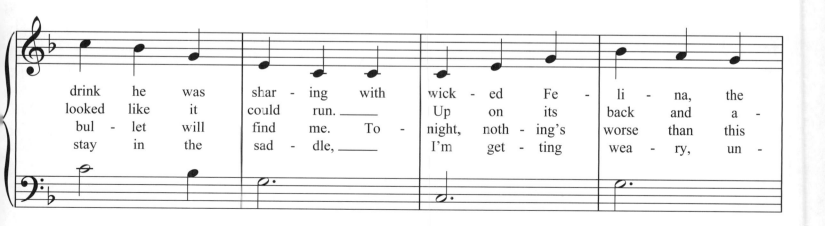

F **G** **G7**

girl that I | loved. _____ | So, in an | - ger, | I
way I did | ride _____ | just as fast | as | I
pain in my | heart. _____ | And at last, | here | I
a - ble to | ride. _____ | But my love | for | Fe -

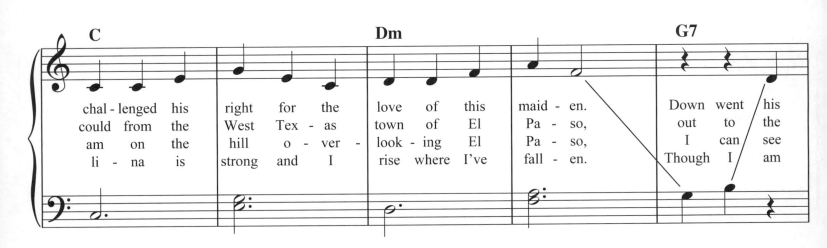

C **Dm** **G7**

chal - lenged his | right for the | love of this | maid - en. | Down went his
could from the | West Tex - as | town of El | Pa - so, | I can see
am on the | hill o - ver - | look - ing El | Pa - so, | Though I am
li - na is | strong and I | rise where I've | fall - en. | out to the

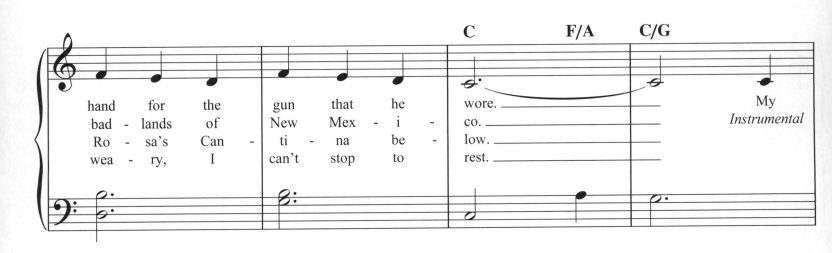

C **F/A** **C/G**

hand for the | gun that he | wore. _____ | My
bad - lands of | New Mex - i - | co. _____ | *Instrumental*
Ro - sa's Can - | ti - na be - | low. _____ |
wea - ry, I | can't stop to | rest. _____ |

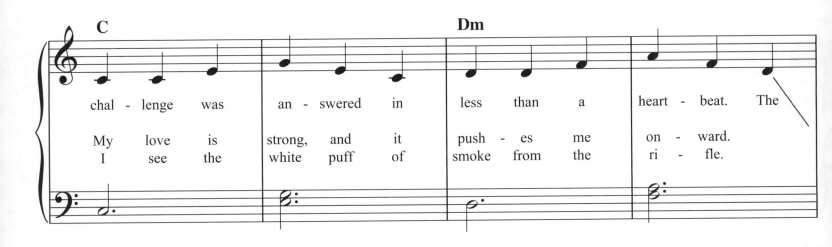

C **Dm**

chal - lenge was | an - swered in | less than a | heart - beat. The
My love is | strong, and it | push - es me | on - ward.
I see the | white puff of | smoke from the | ri - fle.

Play 4 times

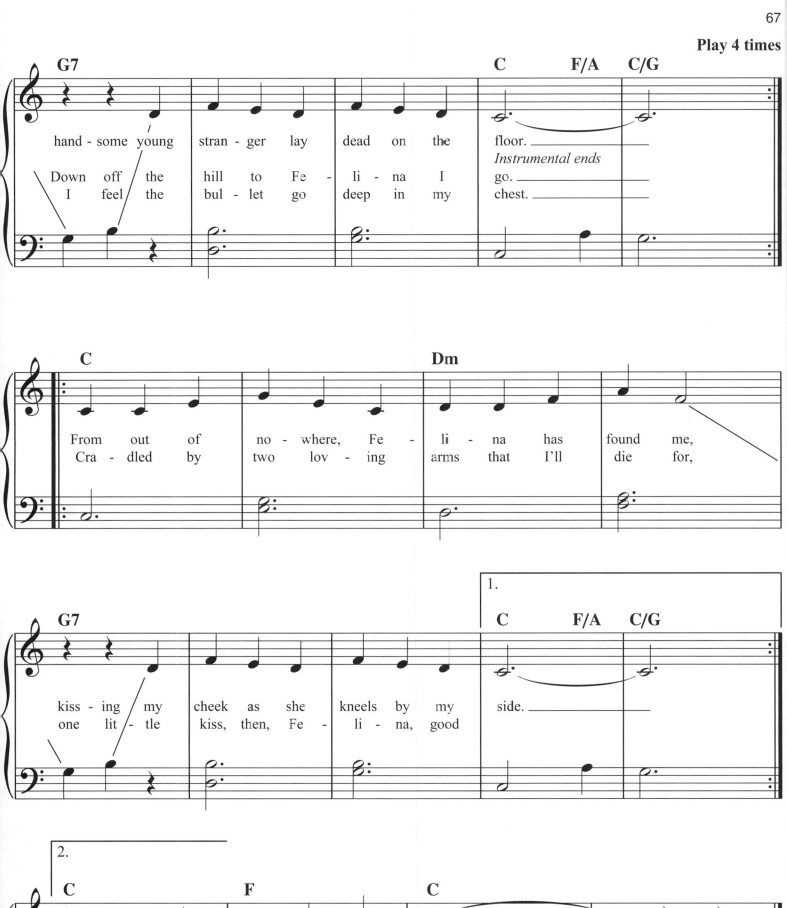

G7   C   F/A   C/G

hand - some young | stran - ger lay | dead on the | floor. _____ |
Instrumental ends
Down off the | hill to Fe - | li - na I | go. _____
I feel the | bul - let go | deep in my | chest. _____

C   Dm

From out of | no - where, Fe - | li - na has | found me,
Cra - dled by | two lov - ing | arms that I'll | die for,

1.

G7   C   F/A   C/G

kiss - ing my | cheek as she | kneels by my | side. _____
one lit - tle | kiss, then, Fe - | li - na, good |

2.

C   F   C

bye.

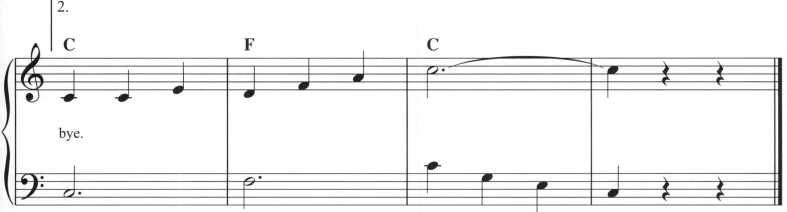

FOLSOM PRISON BLUES

Words and Music by
JOHN R. CASH

Moderately

1. I

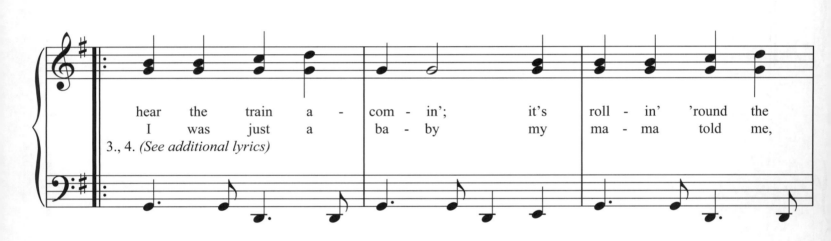

hear the train a - com - in'; it's roll - in' 'round the
I was just a ba - by my ma - ma told me,

3., 4. *(See additional lyrics)*

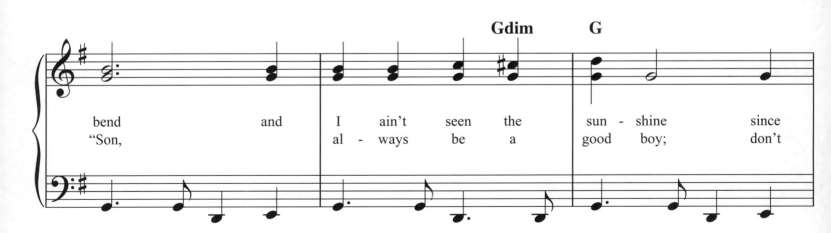

bend and I ain't seen the sun - shine since
"Son, al - ways be a good boy; don't

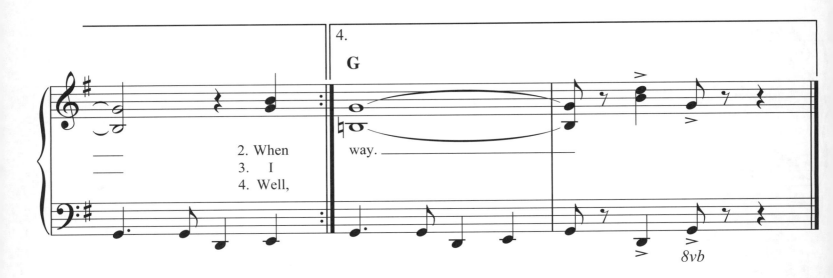

Additional Lyrics

3. I bet there's rich folks eatin' in a fancy dining car.
   They're prob'ly drinkin' coffee and smokin' big cigars.
   But I know I had it comin', I know I can't be free,
   But those people keep a-movin', and that's what tortures me.

4. Well, if they freed me from this prison, if that railroad train was mine,
   I bet I'd move on over a little farther down the line.
   Far from Folsom Prison, that's where I want to stay,
   And I'd let that lonesome whistle blow my blues away.

FOR THE GOOD TIMES

Words and Music by
KRIS KRISTOFFERSON

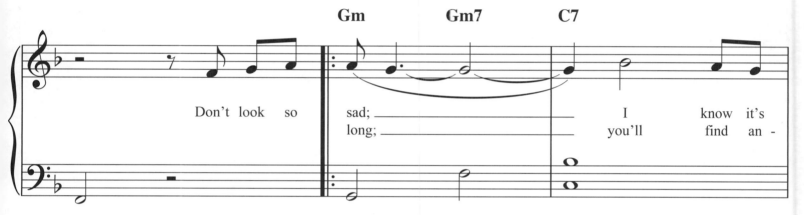

Don't look so sad; _____ I know it's
long; _____ you'll find an -

o - ver; _____ but life goes on _____ and this old
oth - er; _____ and I'll be here _____ if you should

world _____ will keep on turn - ing. _____ Let's just be
find _____ you ev - er need me. _____ Don't say a

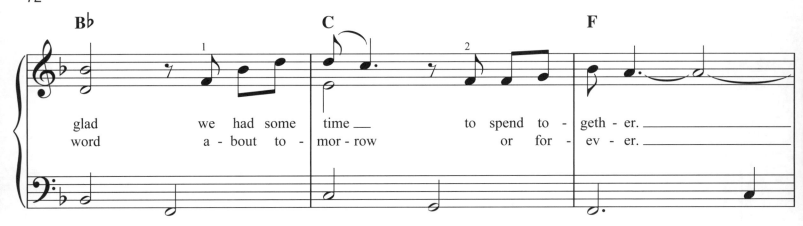

glad   we had some   time ___   to spend to - geth - er. ___
word   a - bout to - mor - row   or for - ev - er. ___

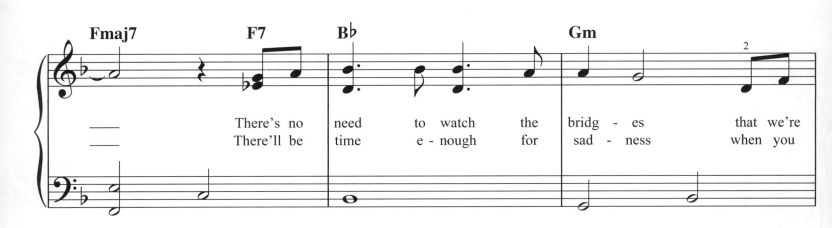

___   There's no   need   to watch   the   bridg - es   that we're
___   There'll be   time   e - nough   for   sad - ness   when you

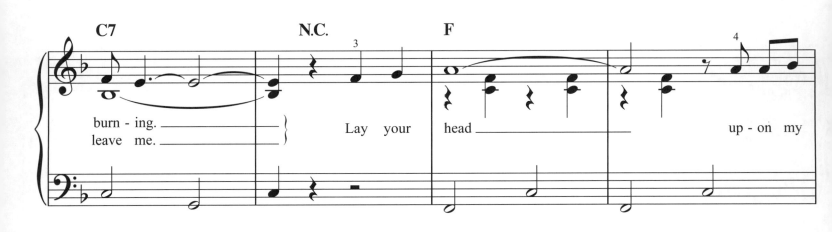

burn - ing. ___   Lay   your   head ___   up - on my
leave me. ___

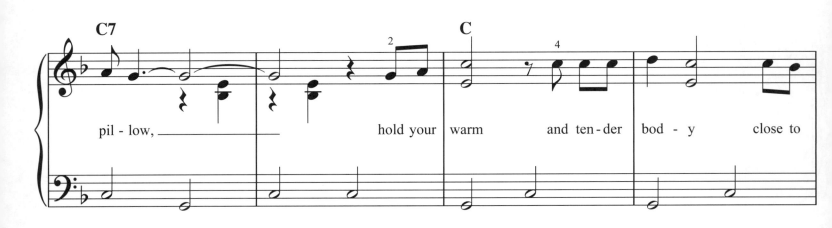

pil - low, ___   hold your warm   and ten - der bod - y   close to

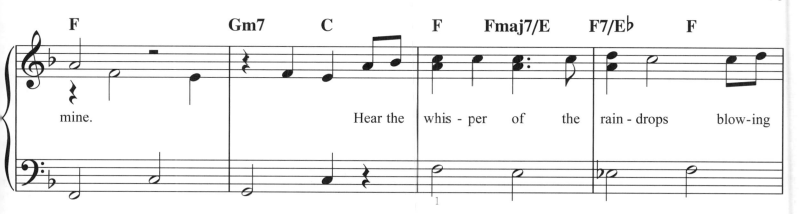

mine.   Hear the   whis - per   of   the   rain - drops   blow-ing

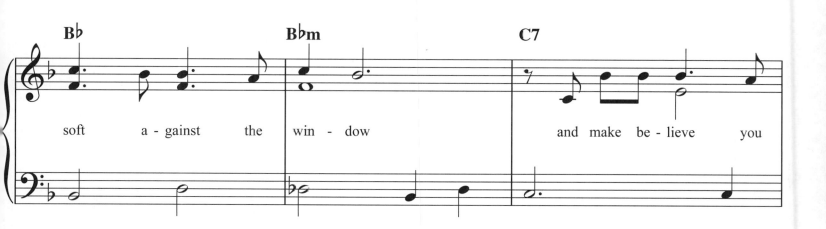

soft   a - gainst   the   win - dow   and make be - lieve   you

love me   one more time, _____   for the

good times. _____   I'll get a - good times. _____

FOREVER AND EVER, AMEN

Words and Music by PAUL OVERSTREET
and DON SCHLITZ

Lively Country

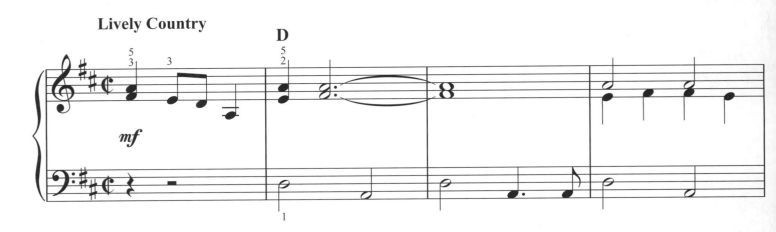

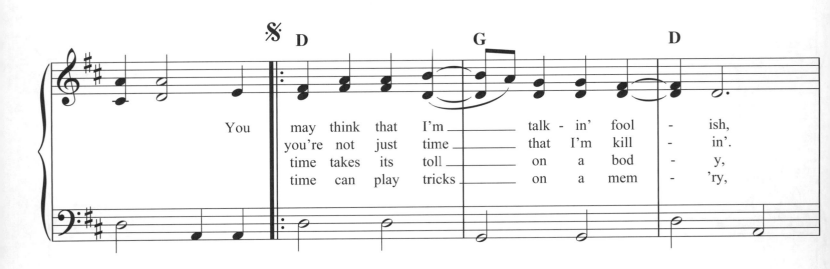

You may think that I'm _____ talk - in' fool - ish,
you're not just time _____ that I'm kill - in'.
time takes its toll _____ on a bod - y,
time can play tricks _____ on a mem - 'ry,

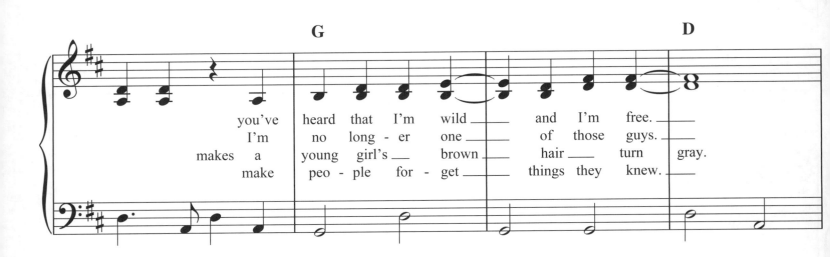

you've heard that I'm wild _____ and I'm free.
I'm no long - er one _____ of those guys.
makes a young girl's _____ brown _____ hair _____ turn gray.
make peo - ple for - get _____ things they knew.

You may won - der how I can
As sure as I live this
Well, hon - ey I don't care, I ain't in
Well, it's eas - y to see, it's

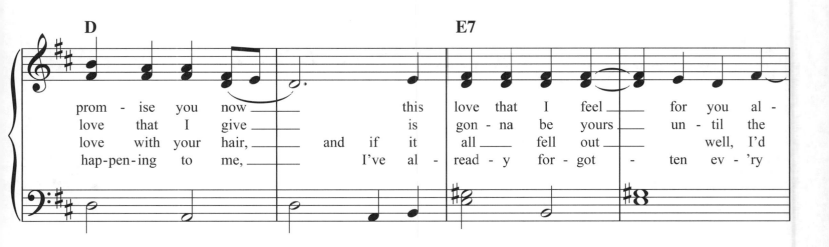

prom - ise you now this love that I feel for you al -
love that I give is gon - na be yours un - til the
love with your hair, and if it all fell out well, I'd
hap - pen - ing to me, I've al - read - y for - got - ten ev - 'ry

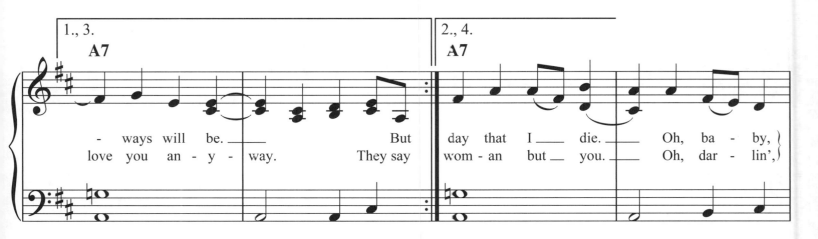

1., 3.
A7
- ways will be. But
love you an - y - way. They say

2., 4.
A7
day that I die. Oh, ba - by,
wom - an but you. Oh, dar - lin',

D G D
I'm gon - na love you for - ev - er, for -

ev - er and ev - er, a - men. _____ As

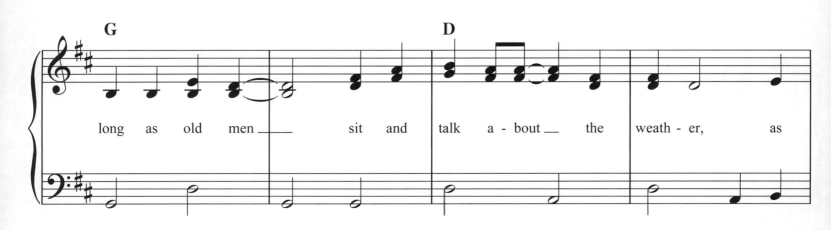

long as old men _____ sit and talk a - bout _____ the weath - er, as

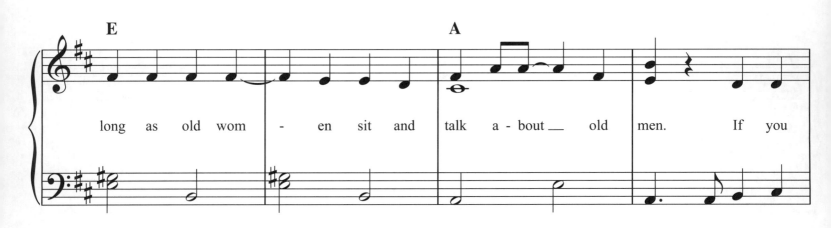

long as old wom - en sit and talk a - bout _____ old men. If you

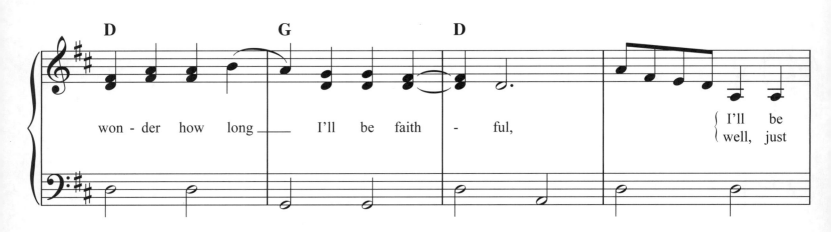

won - der how long _____ I'll be faith - ful, { I'll be
{ well, just

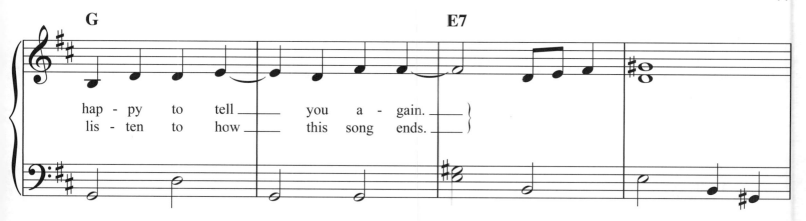

hap - py to tell ___ you a - gain. ___
lis - ten to how ___ this song ends. ___

I'm gon - na love ___ you for - ev - er and ev - er, for -

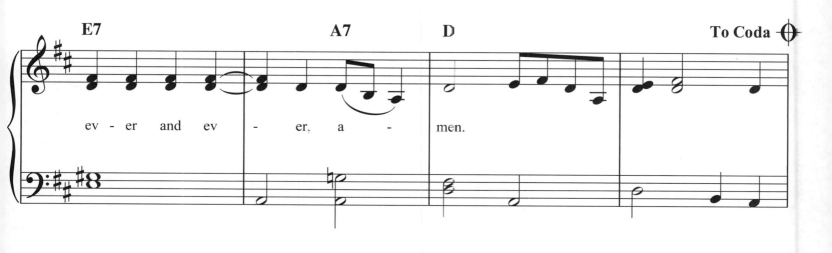

ev - er and ev - er, a - men.

To Coda

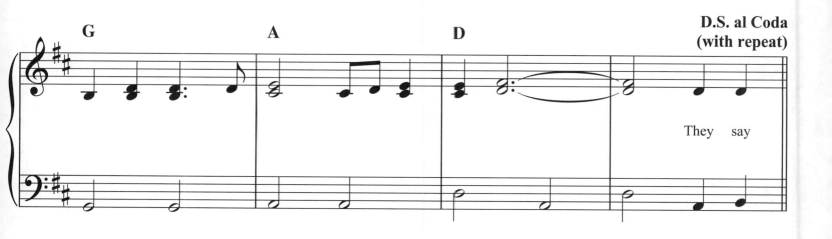

D.S. al Coda
(with repeat)

They say

CODA

I'm gon - na love _____ you for - ev - er and ev -

- er, for - ev - er and ev - er, for -

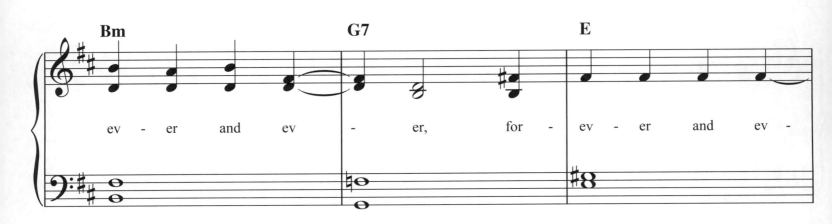

ev - er and ev - er, for - ev - er and ev -

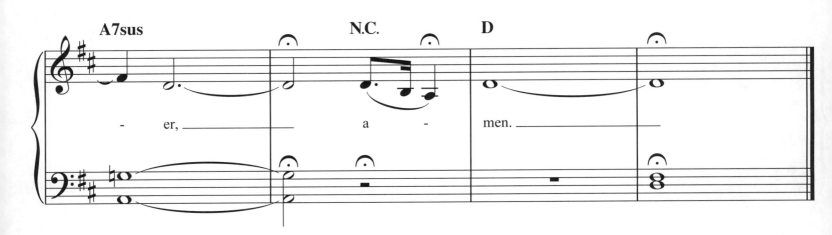

- er, _____ a - men. _____

FRIENDS IN LOW PLACES

Words and Music by DEWAYNE BLACKWELL
and EARL BUD LEE

Moderately, with a beat

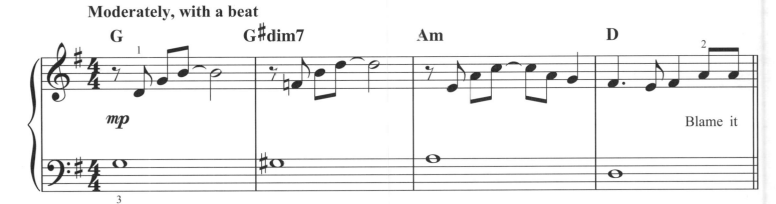

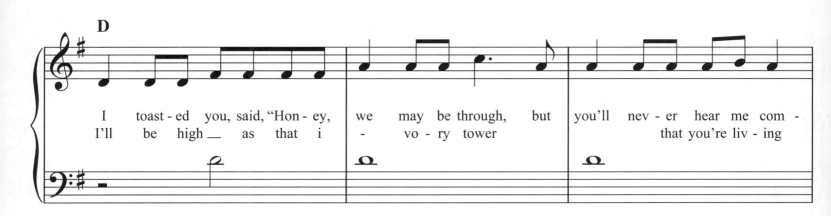

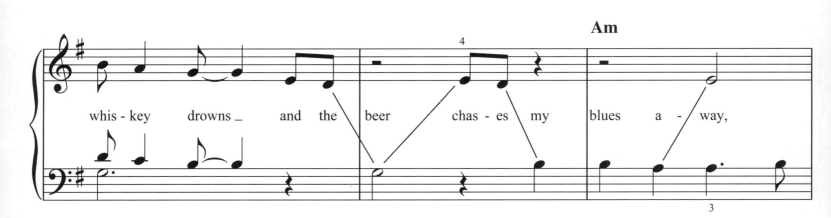

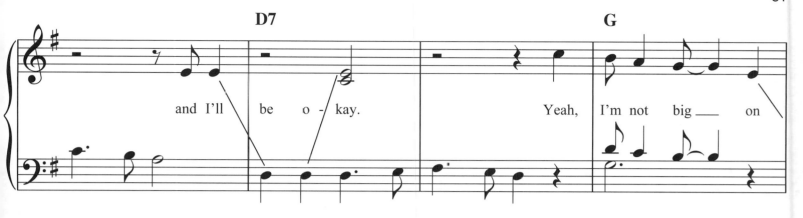

D7　　　　　　　　　　　**G**

and I'll　be　o - kay.　　　　　Yeah,　I'm not　big ___ on

so - cial　grac - es. Think I'll　slip on ___ down　to　the　O - a - sis. Oh, ___

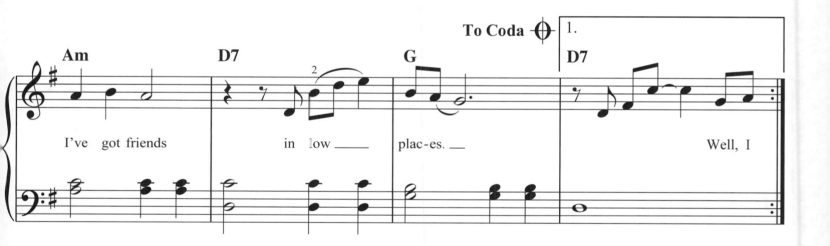

Am　　　**D7**　　　**G**　　To Coda ⊕ | 1. **D7**

I've　got friends　　in　low ___ plac-es. ___　　　　　Well, I

2. **D7**　　　**D.S. al Coda**

Yeah,

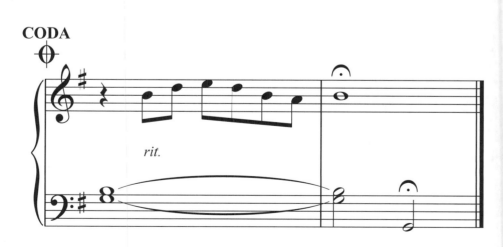

CODA ⊕

rit.

FUNNY HOW TIME SLIPS AWAY

Words and Music by
WILLIE NELSON

long now _____ yet it seems like it was on - ly yes-ter-
same thing _____ that you told me, seems like on - ly yes-ter-
mem - ber _____ what I tell you, that in time _____ you're gon - na

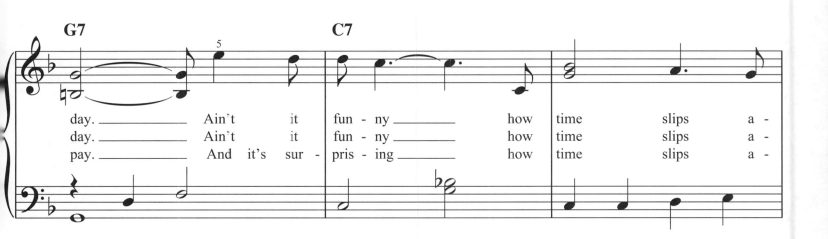

day. _____ Ain't it fun - ny _____ how time slips a -
day. _____ Ain't it fun - ny _____ how time slips a -
pay. _____ And it's sur - pris - ing _____ how time slips a -

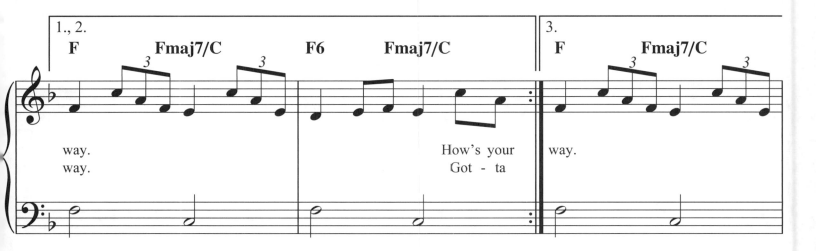

way.
way.

How's your way.
Got - ta

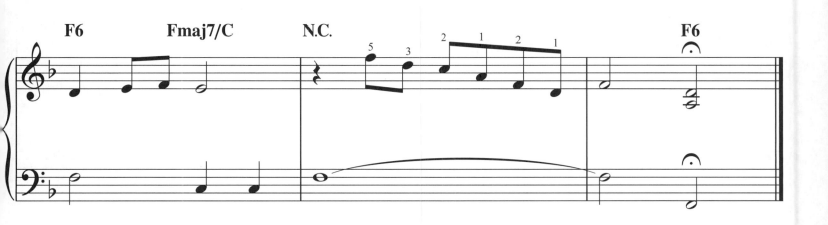

GOD BLESS THE U.S.A.

Words and Music by
LEE GREENWOOD

And I'm proud to be an A-mer-i-can____ where at

least I know I'm free. And I won't for-get the men who died, who

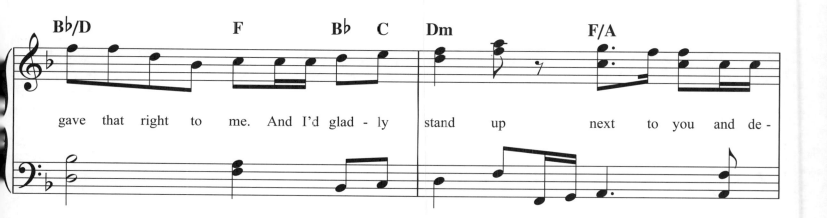

gave that right to me. And I'd glad-ly stand up next to you and de-

To Coda

fend her still to-day, 'cause there ain't no doubt I love this land,____

God bless the U. S. A.

From the

lakes of Min - ne - so - ta to the hills of Ten - nes - see, ___ a -

cross the plains of Tex - as, from sea to shin - ing sea, ___ from

A GOOD HEARTED WOMAN

Words and Music by WILLIE NELSON
and WAYLON JENNINGS

Quickly, in 2

long   time   for - got - ten   are   the   dreams   that   just   fell   by   the
He   likes   the   night - life,   are   the   dreams   bright   lights   and   good - tim - in'

way.   And the
friends.   When the

good   life   he   prom - ised   ain't   what   she's   liv - ing _____ to -
par - ty's   all   o - ver,   she'll   wel - come   him   back   home   a -

F

day. ___
gain. ___
But she
Lord knows she

F7

nev - er com - plains of the bad times or bad things he's
don't un - der - stand him, but ___ she does the best that she

B♭

done, Lord.
can.
She just
'Cause she's a

C7

talks a - bout the good times they've had and all the good times to
good - heart - ed wom - an, she loves her good - tim - in'

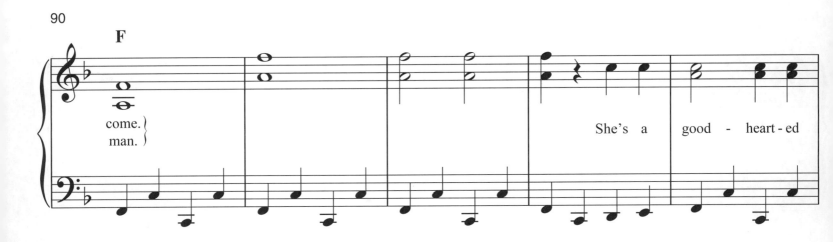

come.
man.

She's a good - heart-ed

F7 **Bb**

wom - an in love with a good - tim - in' man.

C7

She loves him in spite of his

F

ways that she don't un - der - stand.

Through tear - drops and laugh - ter, they'll pass through this

world hand in hand,

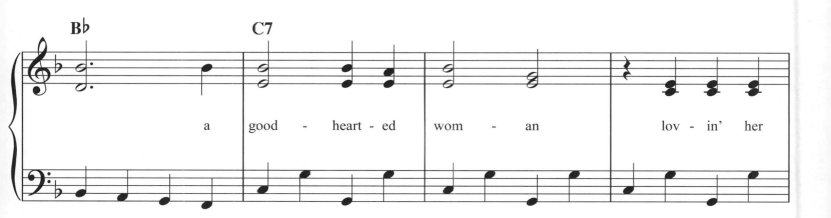

a good - heart - ed wom - an lov - in' her

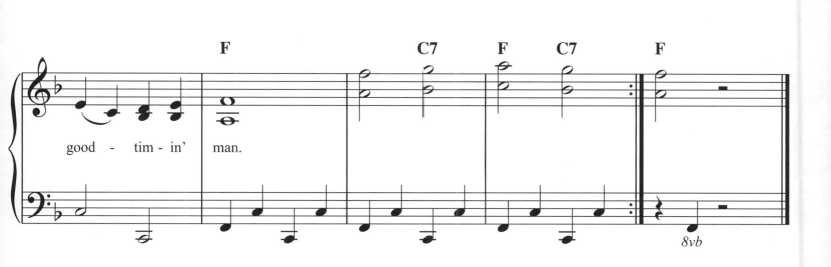

good - tim - in' man.

GRANDPA
(Tell Me 'Bout the Good Old Days)

Words and Music by
JAMIE O'HARA

Medium slow Country

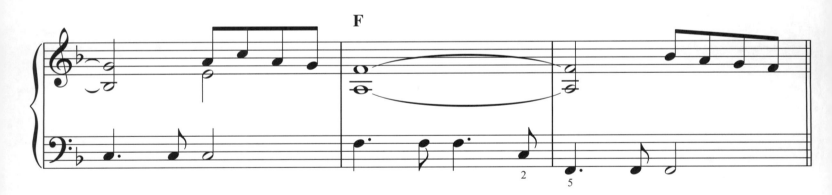

Grand - pa, _____ tell me 'bout the good old days. _
Grand - pa, _____ ev - 'ry - thing is chang - in' fast. _

Some-times _____ it feels like this world's gone cra -
We call _____ it pro - gress, but I just don't know. _

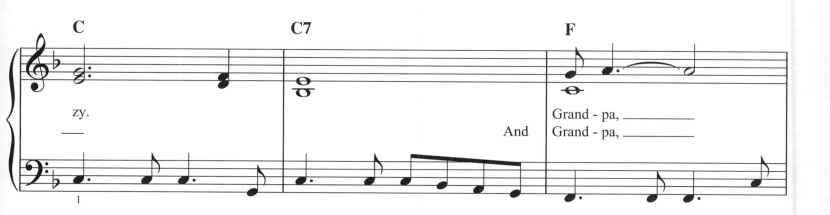

zy.
_____ And Grand - pa, _____
Grand - pa, _____

take me back to yes - ter - day _____ when the line _____ be-tween
let's wan - der back in - to the past. _____ Then _ paint me _____ the

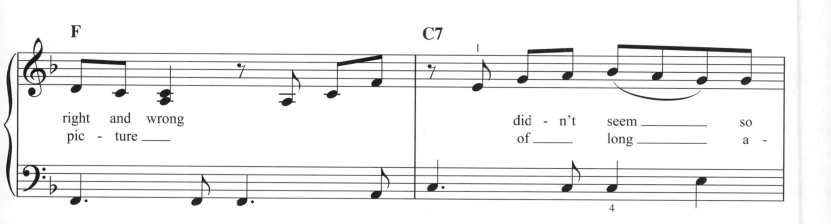

right and wrong did - n't seem _____ so
pic - ture _____ of _____ long _____ a -

ha - zy.
go. ___

Did lov - ers real - ly fall in love to

stay, and stand be - side each oth – er come what may? Was a prom - ise real - ly

some - thing peo - ple ___ kept, not just some-thing they would say? ___

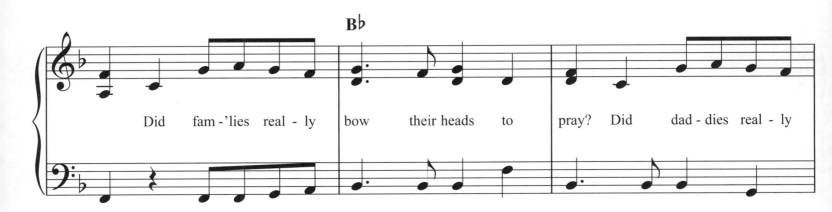

Did fam -'lies real - ly bow their heads to pray? Did dad - dies real - ly

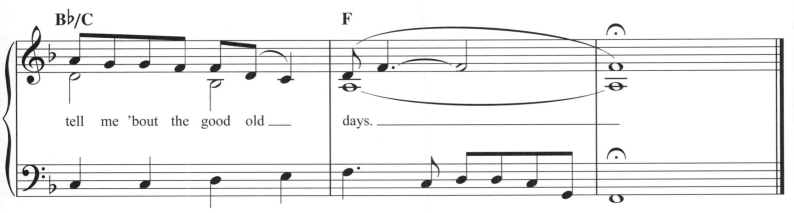

GREEN GREEN GRASS OF HOME

Words and Music by
CURLY PUTMAN

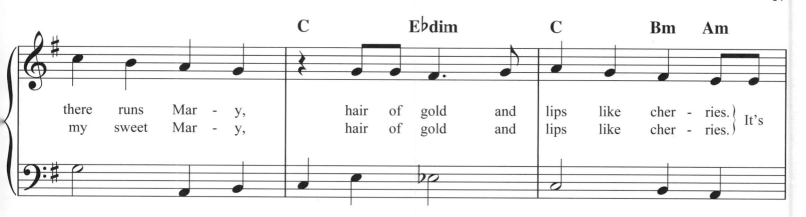

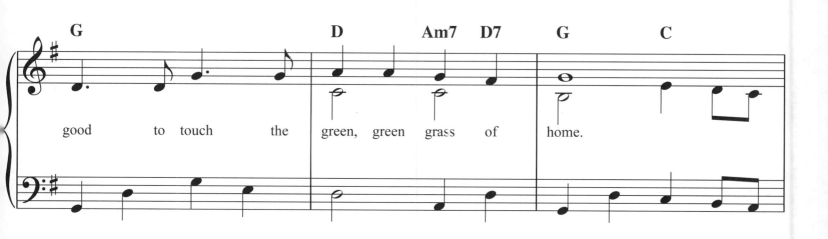

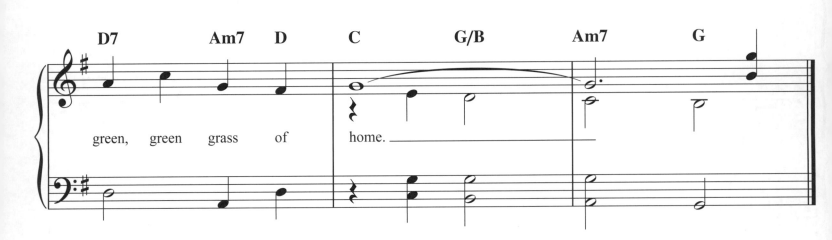

Additional Lyrics

3. Then I awake and look around me
   At four gray walls that surround me,
   And I realize that I was only dreaming.
   For there's a guard and there's a sad old padre,
   Arm in arm we'll walk at daybreak,
   Again I'll touch the green, green grass of home.

   Yes, they'll all come to see me
   In the shade of that old oak tree
   As they lay me 'neath the green, green grass of home.

HEARTACHES BY THE NUMBER

Words and Music by
HARLAN HOWARD

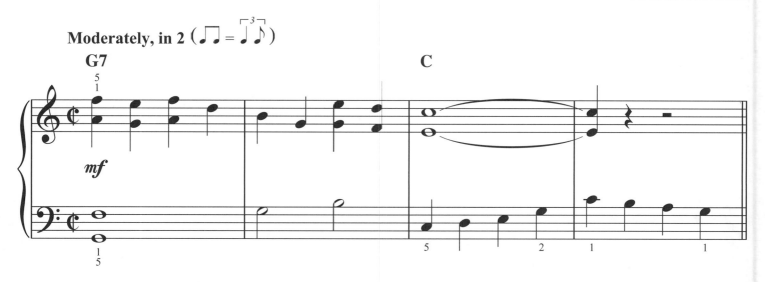

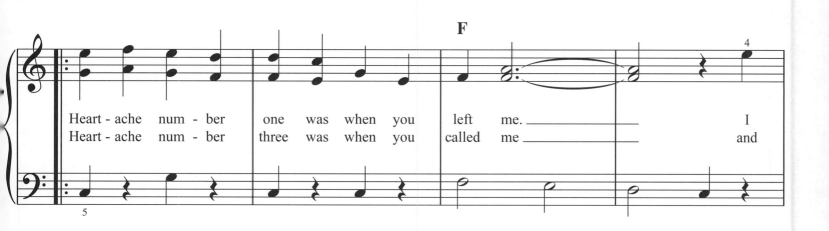

Heart - ache num - ber one was when you left me. _____ I
Heart - ache num - ber three was when you called me _____ and

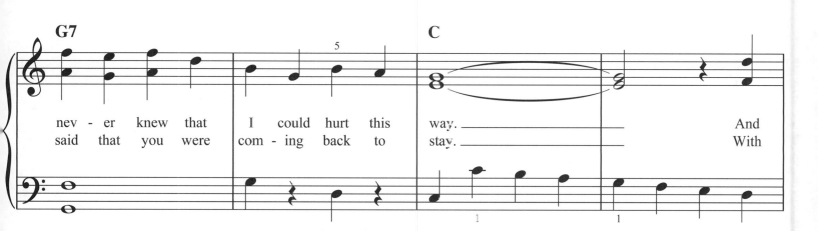

nev - er knew that I could hurt this way. _____ And
said that you were com - ing back to stay. _____ With

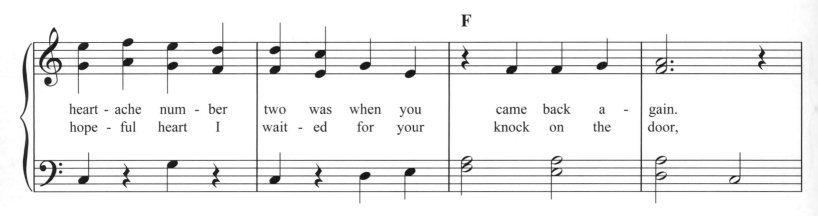

heart - ache num - ber two was when you came back a - gain.
hope - ful heart I wait - ed for your knock on the door,

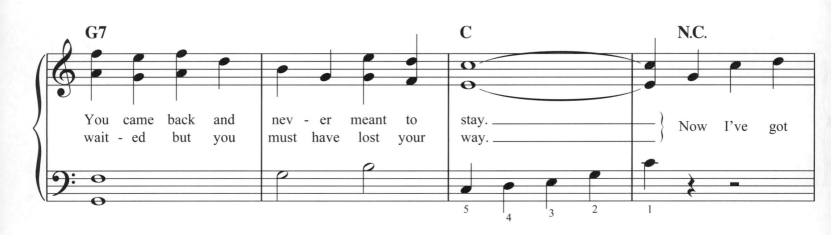

You came back and nev - er meant to stay. _____ Now I've got
wait - ed but you must have lost your way. _____

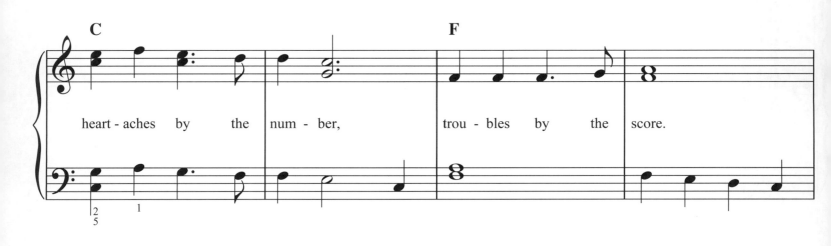

heart - aches by the num - ber, trou - bles by the score.

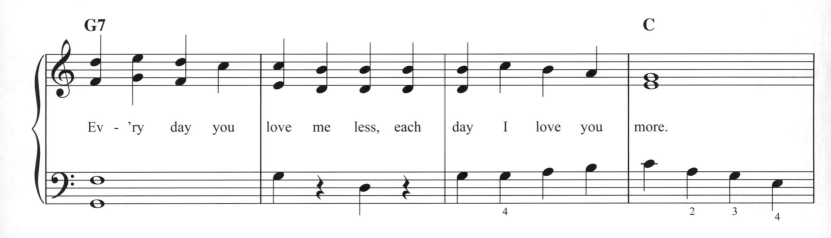

Ev - 'ry day you love me less, each day I love you more.

Yes, I've got heart-aches by the num-ber, a love that I can't

win, but the day that I stop count-ing, that's the day my world will

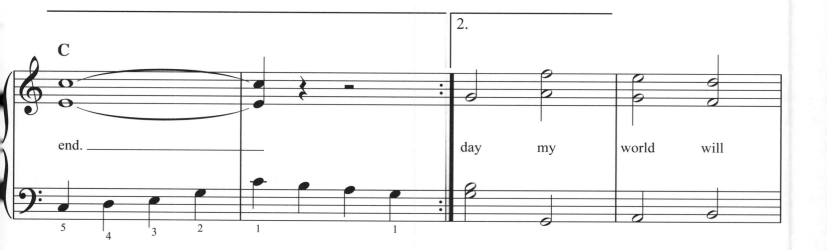

end. _____ day my world will

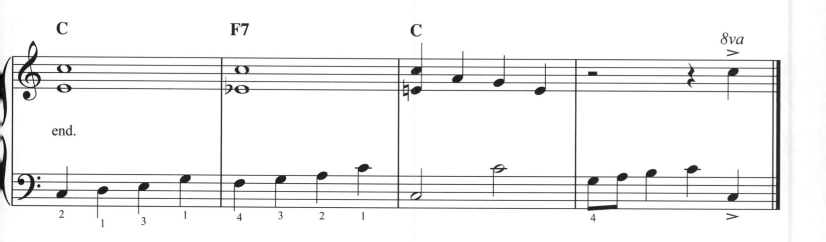

end.

HARPER VALLEY P.T.A.

Words and Music by
TOM T. HALL

Moderately, with a heavy beat

High.
wild.
room.

Well, her daugh-ter came home __ one af-ter-
And we don't be-lieve you ought to be a-
And as she walked up to the black-board, I

noon, and did-n't e-ven stop to play.
bring-ing up your lit-tle girl this way."
still re-call the words she had to say.

She said,
It was
She said, "I'd

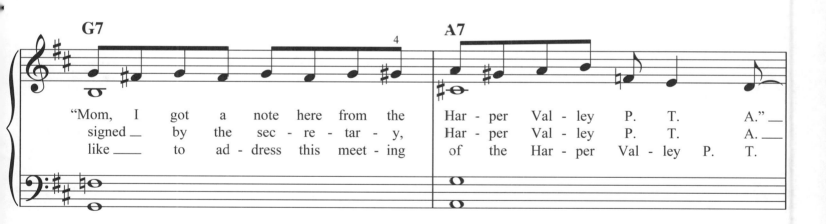

"Mom, I got a note here from the
signed __ by the sec-re-tar-y,
like __ to ad-dress this meet-ing

Har-per Val-ley P. T. A." __
Har-per Val-ley P. T. A. __
of the Har-per Val-ley P. T.

__
A."

The
Well, it

"Well, there's

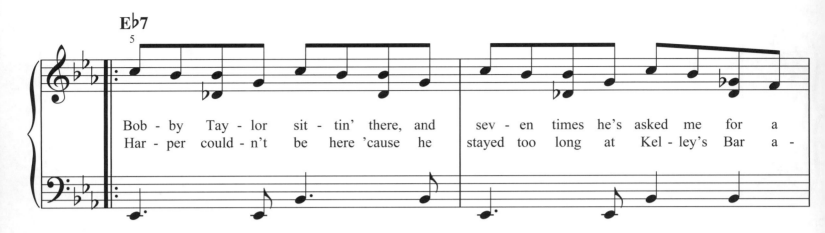

Bob - by Tay - lor sit - tin' there, and sev - en times he's asked me for a
Har - per could - n't be here 'cause he stayed too long at Kel - ley's Bar a -

date. Mis-sus Tay - lor sure seems _ to use a
gain. And if you smell _ Shir - ley Thomp-son's breath, you'll

lot of ice when-ev - er he's a - way. And Mis - ter
find she's had a lit - tle nip of gin. Then you

Bak - er, can you tell us why your sec - re - tar - y had to leave this
have the nerve to tell me ____ you think that as a moth - er I'm not
would - n't put you on be - cause it real - ly did, it hap - pened just this

town? And should-n't wid - ow Jones be told to keep her
fit. Well, this is just a lit - tle Pey - ton Place, and
way, the day my Ma - ma socked it to _____ the

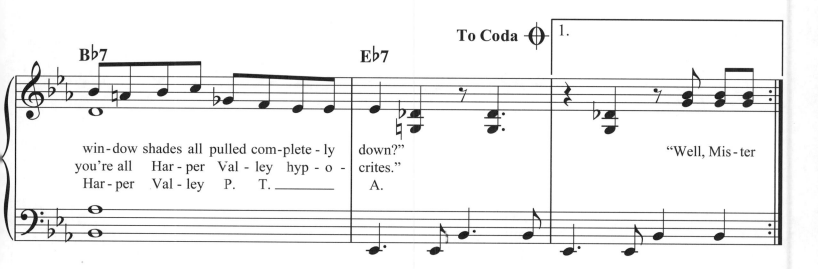

win - dow shades all pulled com - plete - ly down?"
you're all Har - per Val - ley hyp - o - crites."
Har - per Val - ley P. T. _____ A.

"Well, Mis - ter

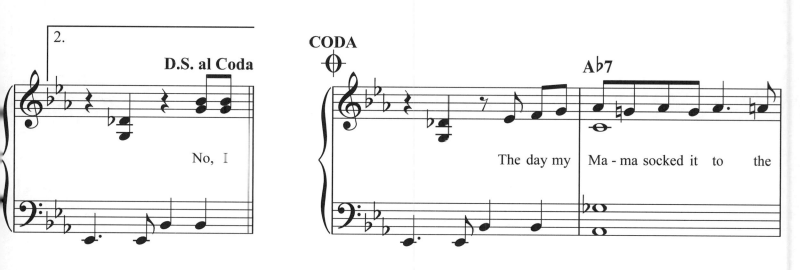

No, I

The day my Ma - ma socked it to the

Har - per Val - ley P. T. A. _____

HELLO WALLS

Words and Music by
WILLIE NELSON

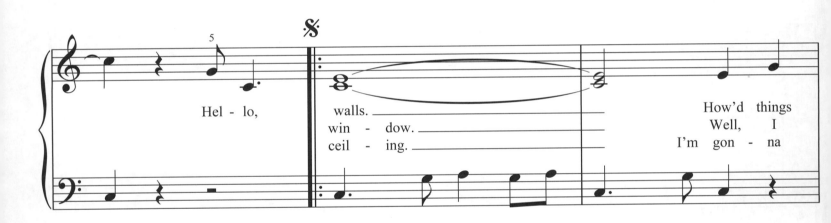

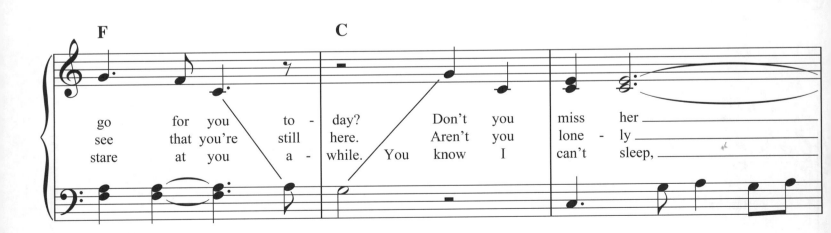

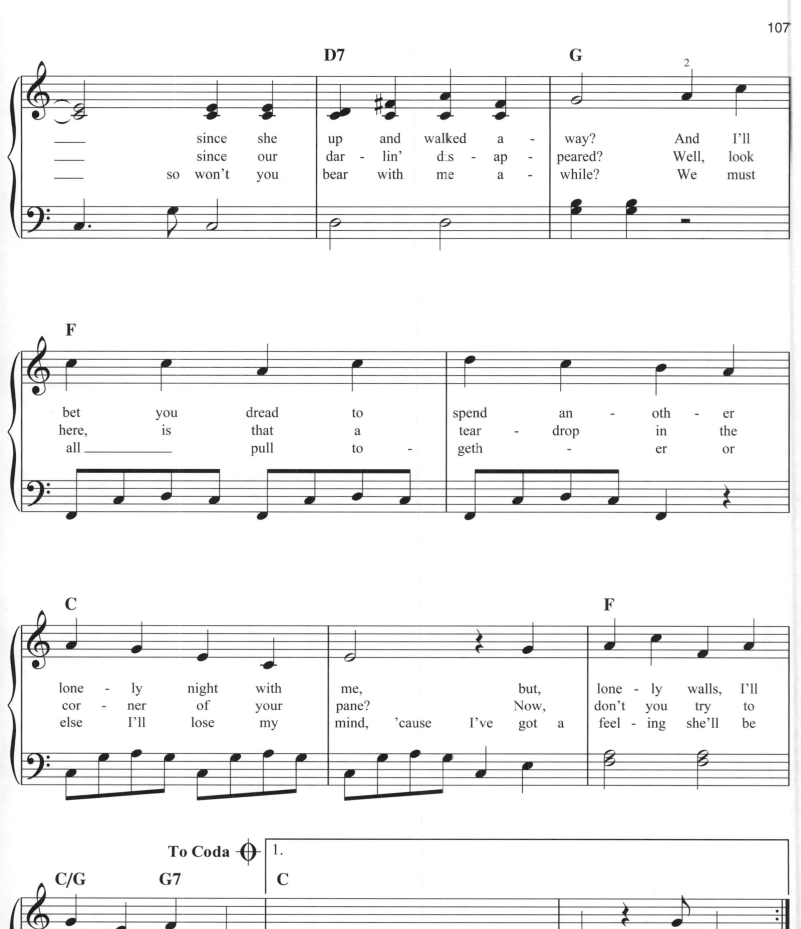

rain. _____

She went a - way and left us

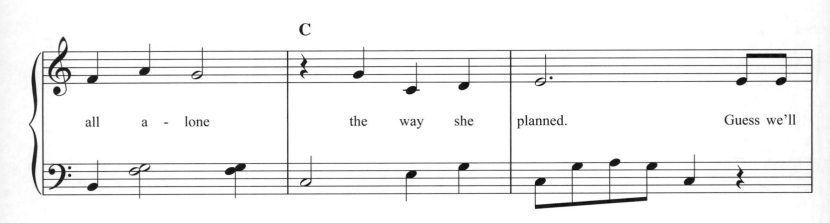

all a - lone the way she planned. Guess we'll

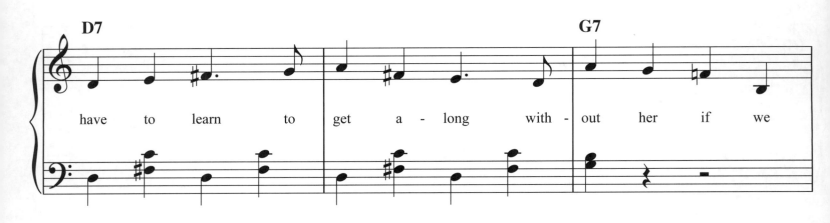

have to learn to get a - long with - out her if we

D.S. al Coda
N.C.

can. Hel - lo,

CODA
C

time. _____

HEY, GOOD LOOKIN'

Words and Music by
HANK WILLIAMS

ba - by,
look - in',   I

don't _____ you think
know _____ I've been

may - be,
took - en.

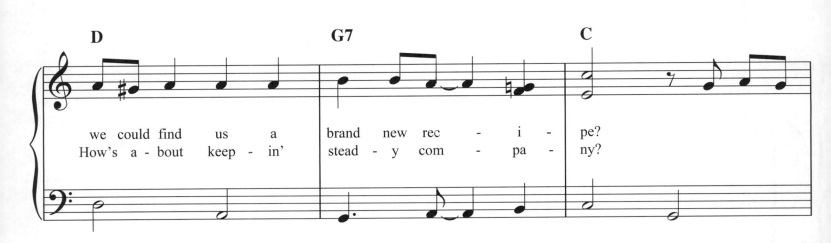

D   **G7**   **C**

we could find   us   a
How's a - bout keep - in'

brand new rec - i - pe?
stead - y com - pa - ny?

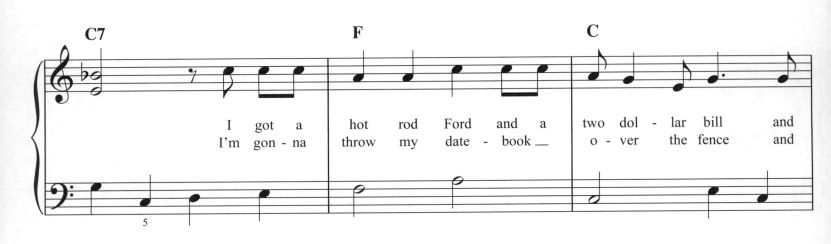

C7   **F**   **C**

I got a
I'm gon - na

hot rod Ford and a
throw my date - book

two dol - lar bill   and
o - ver the fence   and

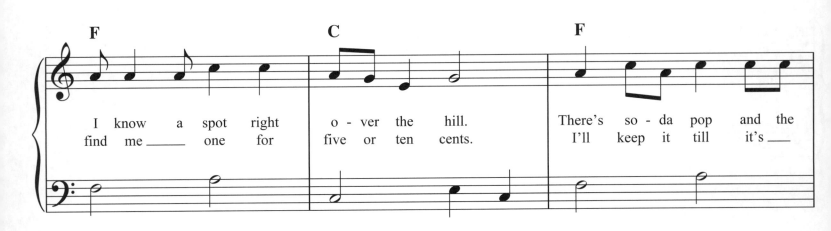

F   **C**   **F**

I know a spot right
find me _____ one for

o - ver the hill.
five or ten cents.

There's so - da pop and the
I'll keep it till it's _____

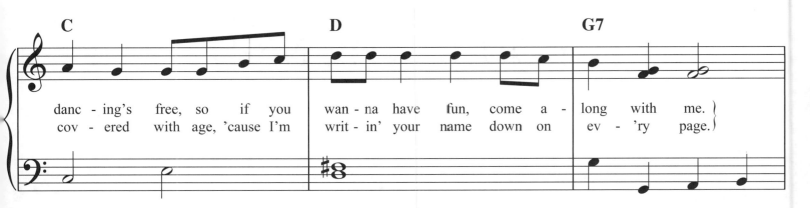

C · D · G7

danc - ing's free, so if you wan - na have fun, come a - long with me.
cov - ered with age, 'cause I'm writ - in' your name down on ev - 'ry page.

C

Hey, good look - in', what - cha got

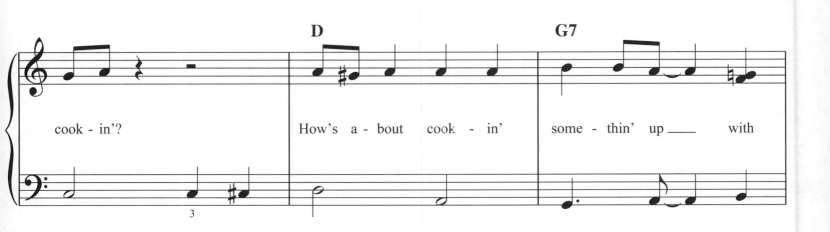

D · G7

cook - in'? How's a - bout cook - in' some - thin' up ___ with

1. C Am Dm7 Gsus7 | 2. C

me? I'm me? rit.

HELP ME MAKE IT THROUGH THE NIGHT

Words and Music by
KRIS KRISTOFFERSON

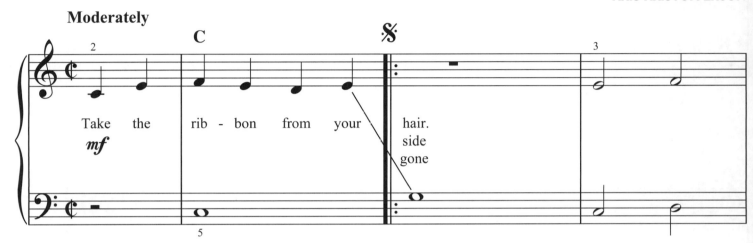

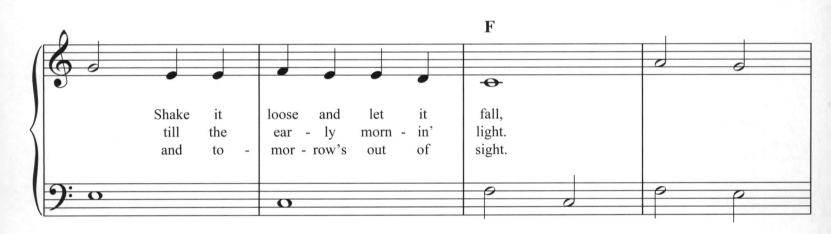

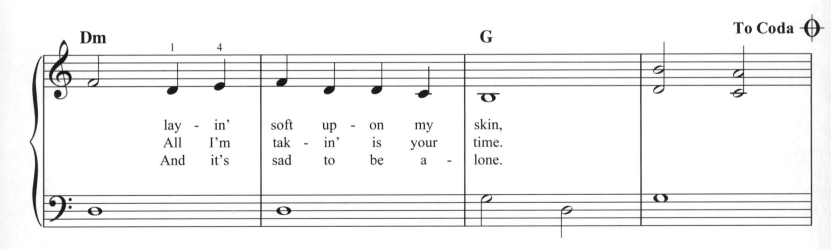

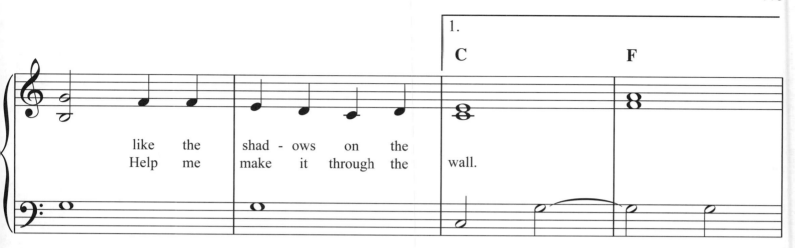

like the   shad - ows   on   the
Help me   make it through the   wall.

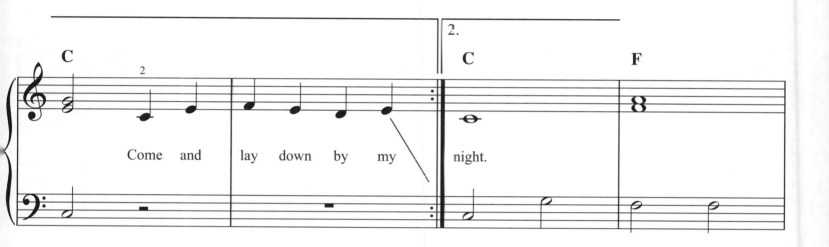

Come   and   lay   down   by   my   night.

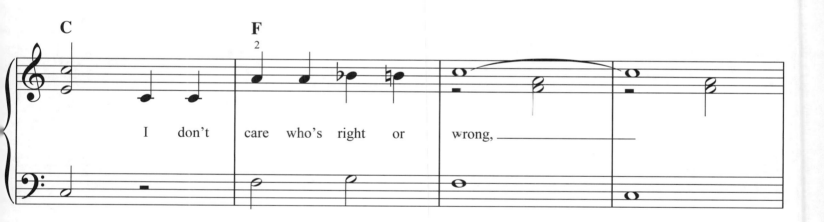

I   don't   care who's right or   wrong, _____

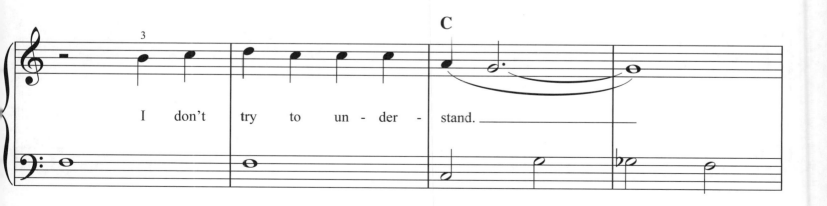

I   don't   try to un - der - stand. _____

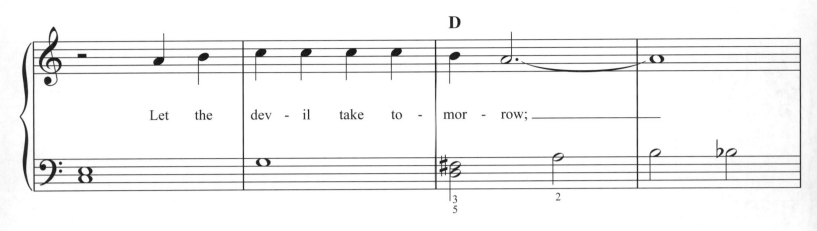

D

Let the dev - il take to - mor - row; _____

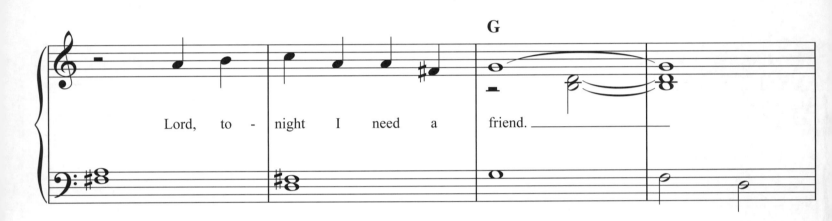

G

Lord, to - night I need a friend. _____

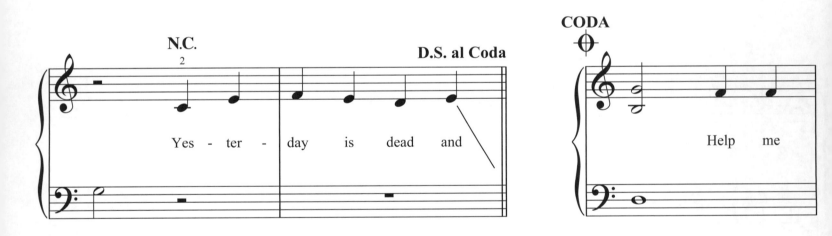

N.C.   **D.S. al Coda**   **CODA**

Yes - ter - day is dead and   Help me

C   **F**   **C**

make it through the night.

I CAN'T HELP IT
(If I'm Still in Love with You)

Words and Music by
HANK WILLIAMS

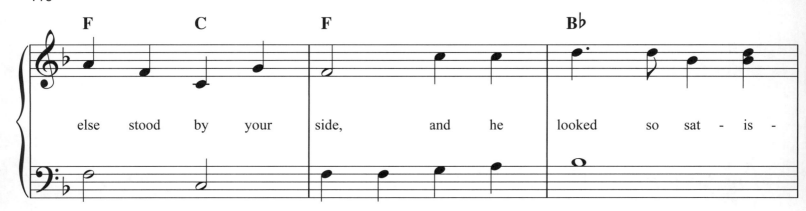

else stood by your side, and he looked so sat - is -

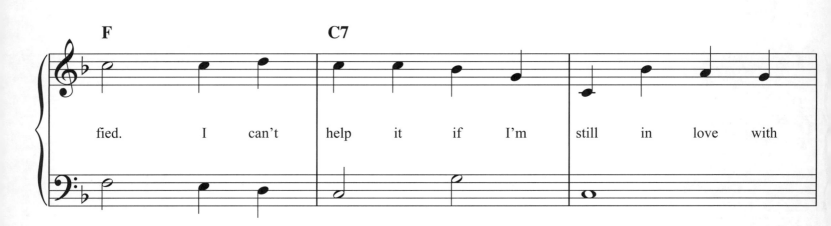

fied. I can't help it if I'm still in love with

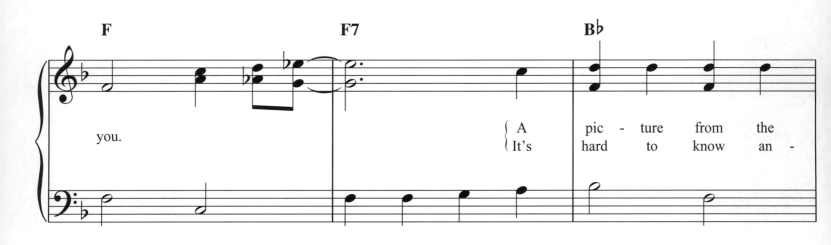

you.

A pic - ture from the
It's hard to know an -

past came slow - ly steal - ing _____ as I
oth - er's lips will kiss you _____ and _____

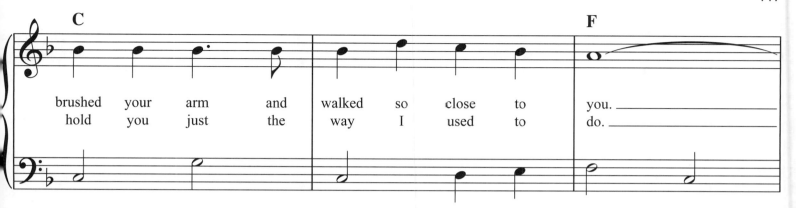

brushed your arm and walked so close to you.
hold you just and the way I used to do.

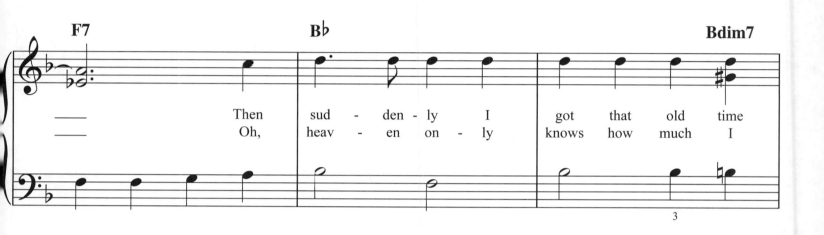

Then sud - den - ly I got that old time
Oh, heav - en on - ly knows how much I

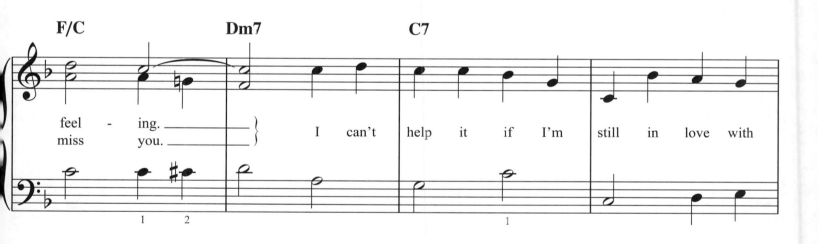

feel - ing. I can't help it if I'm still in love with
miss you.

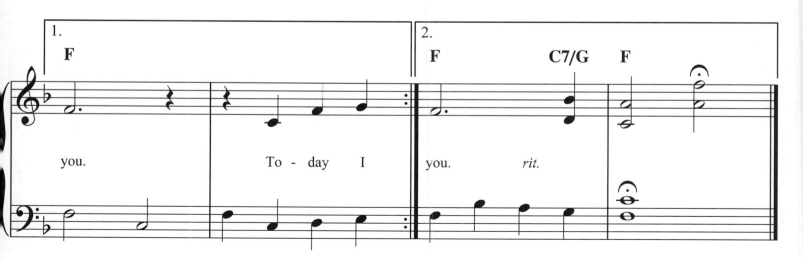

1.
you.   To - day I

2.
you.   *rit.*

(Hey, Won't You Play)

ANOTHER SOMEBODY DONE SOMEBODY WRONG SONG

Words and Music by LARRY BUTLER
and CHIPS MOMAN

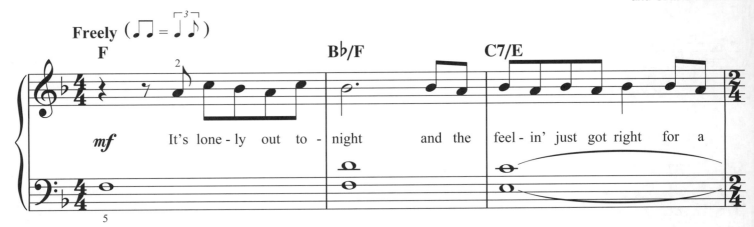

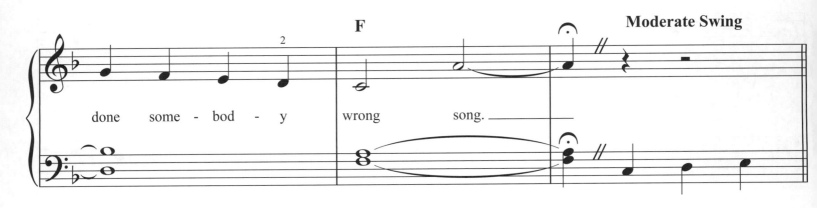

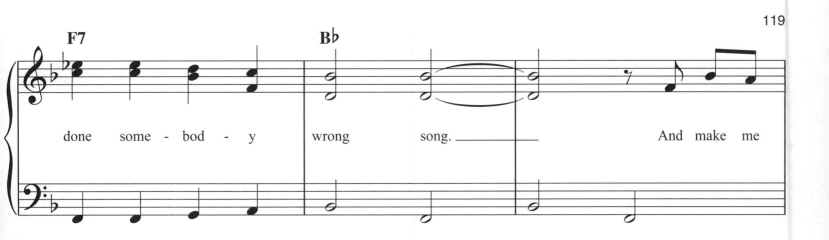

done some - bod - y wrong song. ____ And make me

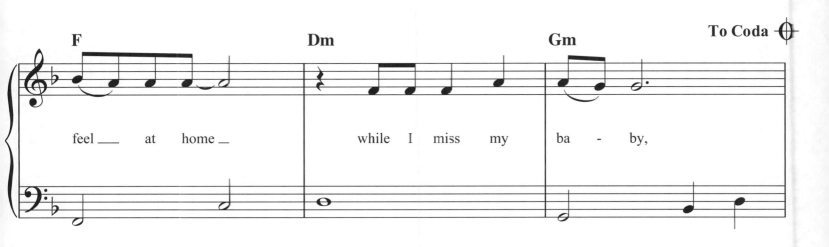

feel ___ at home ___ while I miss my ba - by,

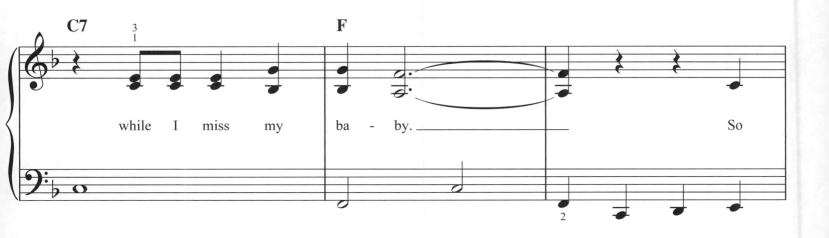

while I miss my ba - by. ____ So

play, play for me a sad mel - o - dy, ___

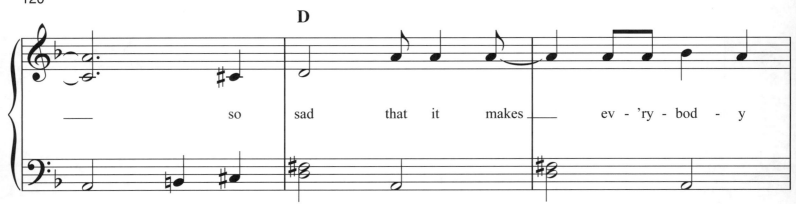

so sad that it makes ev - 'ry - bod - y

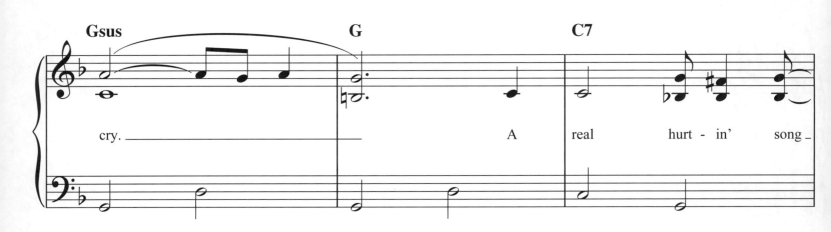

cry. _____ A real hurt - in' song ___

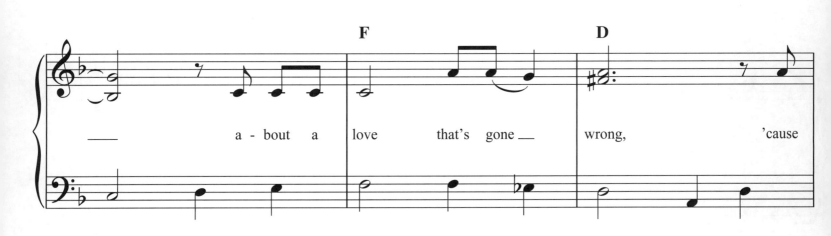

___ a - bout a love that's gone ___ wrong, 'cause

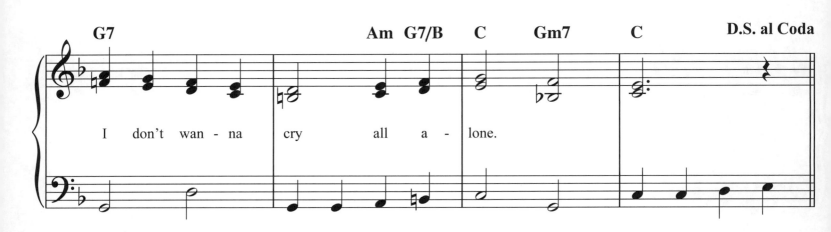

I don't wan - na cry all a - lone.

CODA

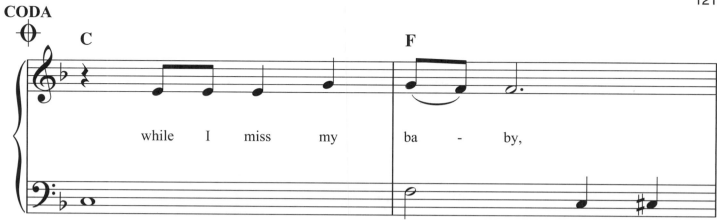

while I miss my ba - by,

while I miss my ba - by, while I miss my

ba - by, while I miss my ba - by,

while I miss my ba - by.

rit.

I CAN'T STOP LOVING YOU

Words and Music by
DON GIBSON

heals ___ a bro - ken heart, but time has stood

still ___ since we've been a - part.

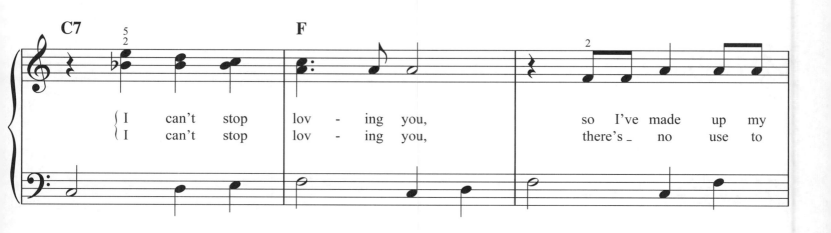

I can't stop lov - ing you, so I've made up my
I can't stop lov - ing you, there's _ no use to

mind ___ to live in mem - o - ry ___
try. ___ Pre - tend there's some - one new; ___

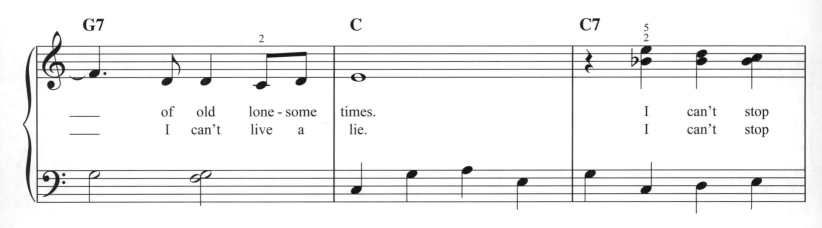

of old lone - some times.
I can't live a lie.
I can't stop
I can't stop

want - ing you,
want - ing you
it's use - less to say,
the way that I do.

so I'll just live my life in dreams of yes - ter -
There's on - ly been one love for me, that one is

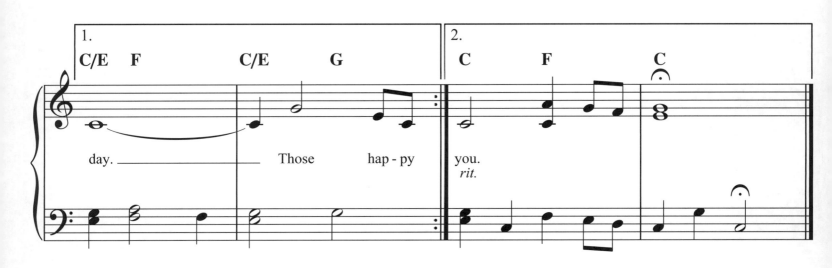

1.
C/E F   C/E   G

day. _____ Those hap - py

2.
C   F   C

you.
rit.

I SAW THE LIGHT

Words and Music by
HANK WILLIAMS

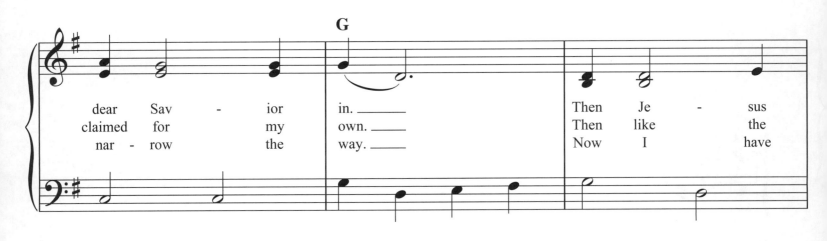

dear Sav - ior in. _____ Then Je - sus
claimed for my own. _____ Then like the
nar - row the way. _____ Now I have

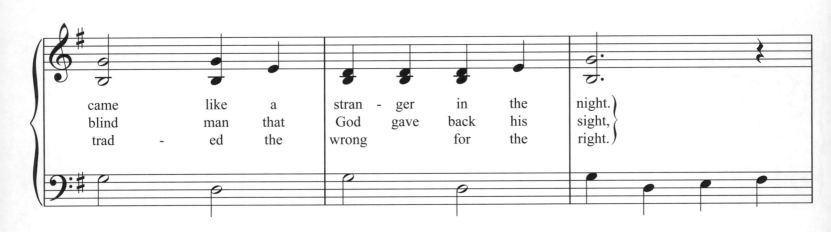

came like a stran - ger in the night.
blind man that God gave back his sight,
trad - ed the wrong for the right.

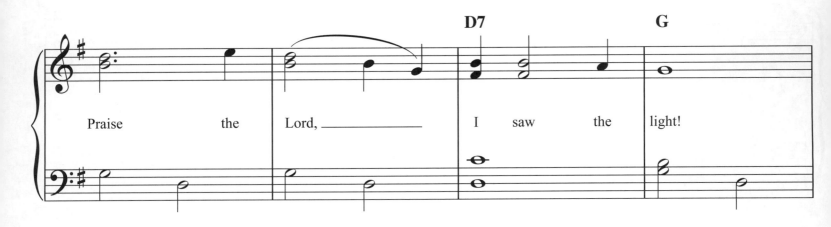

Praise the Lord, _____ I saw the light!

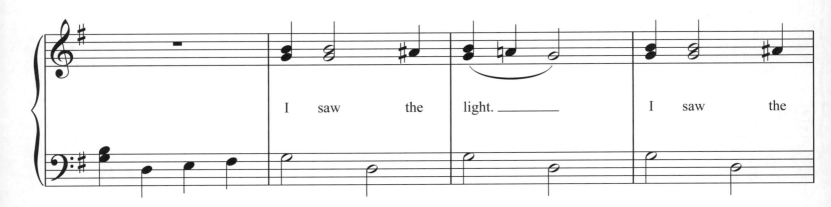

I saw the light. _____ I saw the

light. _____ No more dark - ness, no more

night. _____ Now I'm so hap - py, no sor - row in

sight. _____ Praise the Lord, _____ I saw the

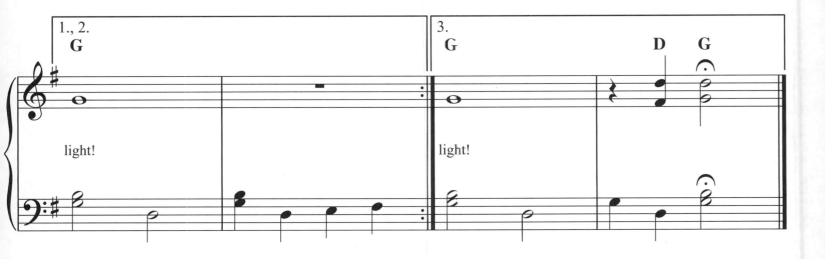

light!   light!

I FALL TO PIECES

Words and Music by HANK COCHRAN
and HARLAN HOWARD

Bb/F   C7

act   like   we've   nev - er   kissed, _____   you   want   me   to   for -
find   some - one   else   to   love, _____   some - one   who'll   love   me

F   Bb

get,   pre-tend   we've   nev - er   met; _____   and   I've   tried _____   and   I've
too   the   way   you   used   to   do; _____   but   each   time _____   I   go

C7   F/A   Bb

tried _____   but   I   have - n't   yet. _____   You   walk   by   and
out   with _   some - one   new, _____   you   walk   by   and

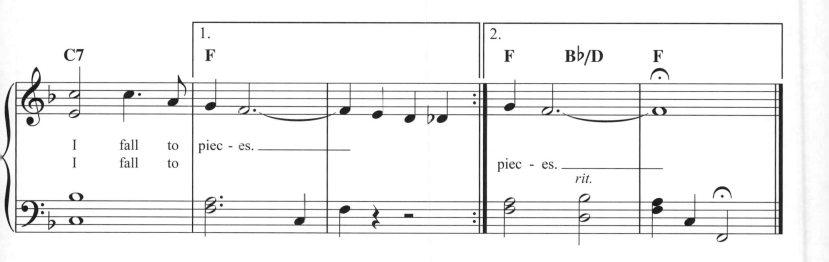

C7   1. F   2. F   Bb/D   F

I   fall   to   piec - es. _____
I   fall   to   piec - es. _____
                                                             rit.

I WILL ALWAYS LOVE YOU

featured in THE BODYGUARD

Words and Music by
DOLLY PARTON

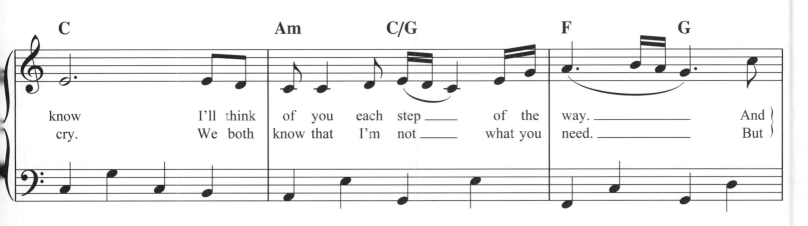

know   I'll think   of   you   each   step _____ of   the   way. _____ And
cry.   We   both   know   that   I'm   not _____ what   you   need. _____ But

I _____ will   al - ways _ love _ you. _____ I _____ will

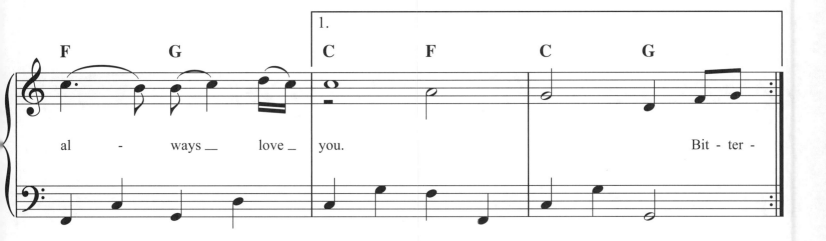

al - ways _ love _ you.   Bit - ter -

you. _____   I   will   al-ways   love   you.

I.O.U.

Words and Music by KERRY CHATER
and AUSTIN ROBERTS

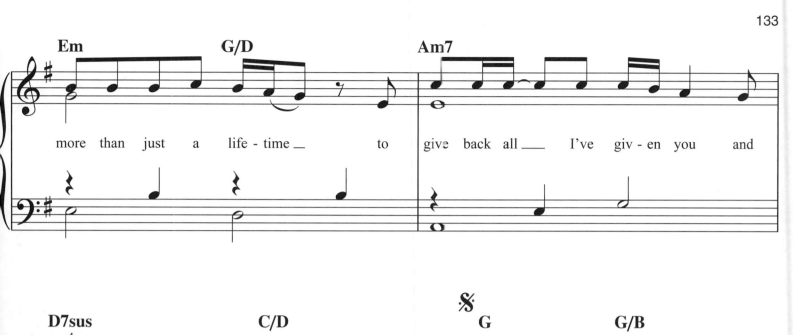

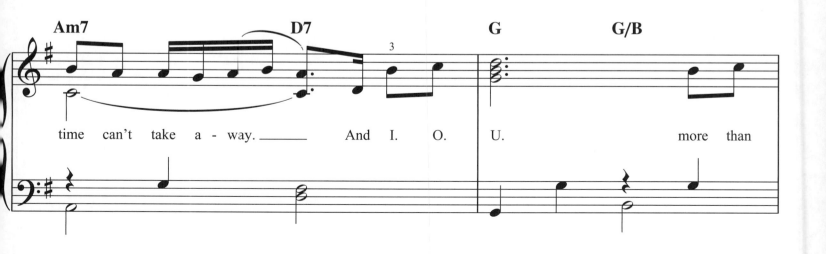

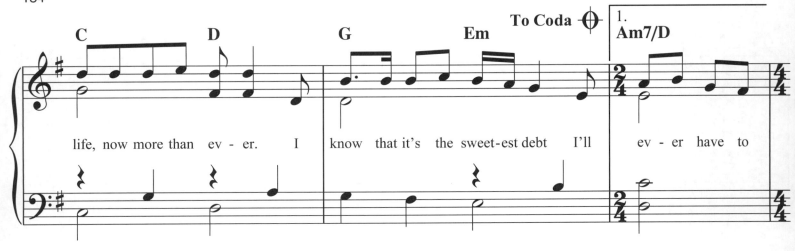

Additional Lyrics

I'm amazed when you say it's me you live for
And you know that when I'm holding you,
You're right where you belong.
And, my love, I can't help but smile with wonder
When you tell me what I've done for you,
'Cause I've known all along that I.O.U.

The sunlight in the morning....

IT WAS ALMOST LIKE A SONG

Lyric by HAL DAVID
Music by ARCHIE JORDAN

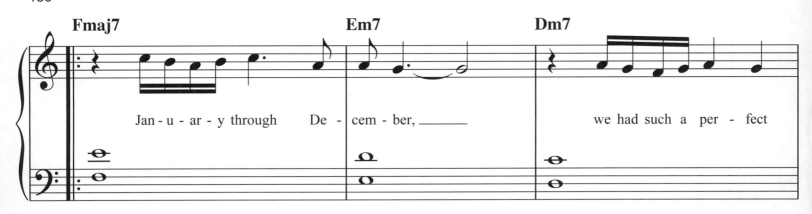

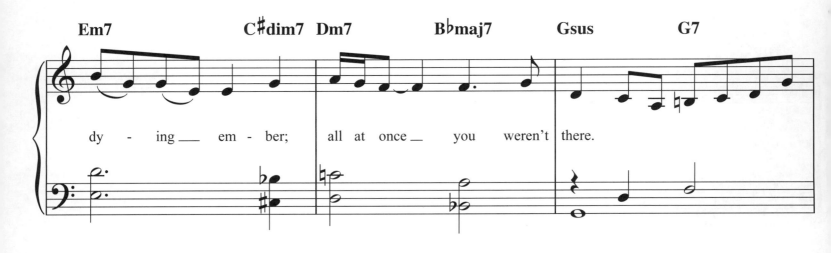

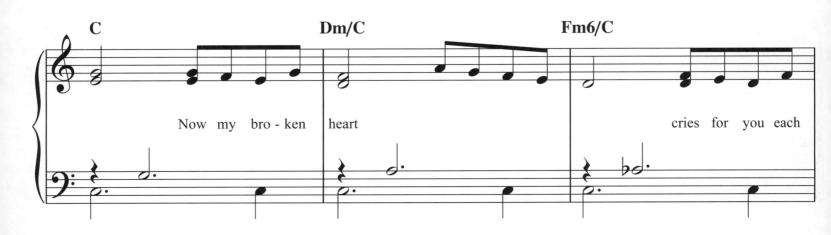

JAMBALAYA
(On the Bayou)

Words and Music by
HANK WILLIAMS

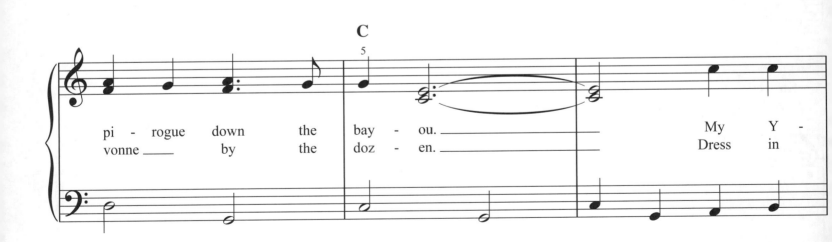

vonne, the sweet - est one, me oh my oh. _____
style and go hog wild, me oh my oh. _____

_____ Son of a gun, we'll have big fun on the
_____ Son of a gun, we'll have big fun on the

bay - ou. ⎫
bay - ou. ⎭   Jam - ba - la - ya and a craw - fish

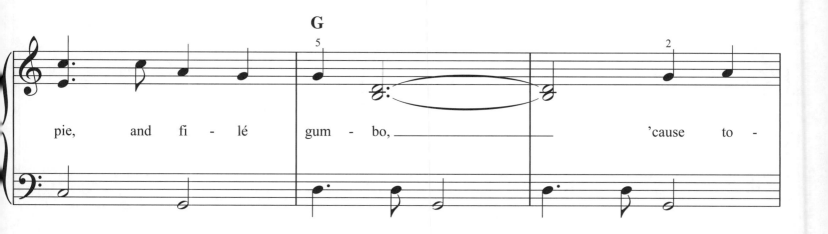

pie, and fi - lé gum - bo, _____ 'cause to -

139

night I'm gon - na see my ma cher a - mi - o. _____

_____ Pick gui - tar, fill fruit jar and be gay - o. _____

_____ Son of a gun we'll have big fun on the

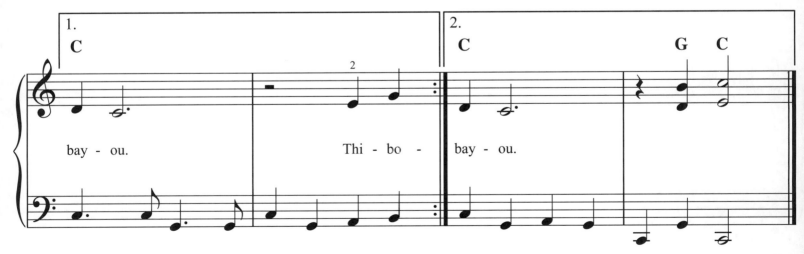

bay - ou.   Thi - bo -   bay - ou.

LAST DATE

By FLOYD CRAMER

142

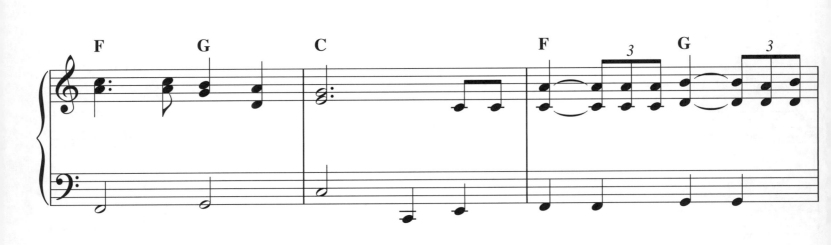

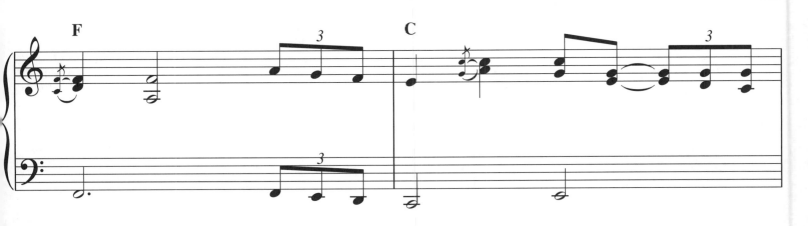

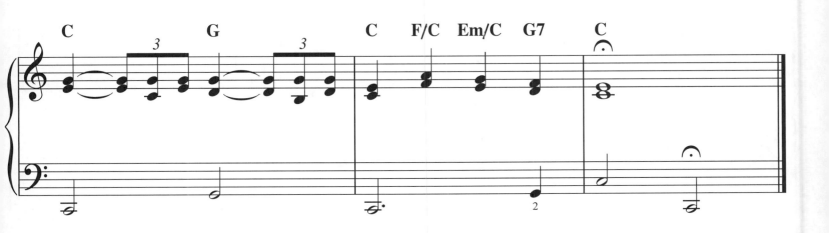

KING OF THE ROAD

Words and Music by
ROGER MILLER

Trail - er for sale or rent, __
Third box - car mid - night train, __

rooms _ to let; fif - ty cents. __
des - ti - na-tion: Ban - gor, Maine. __

No phone, no pool, no pets; __
Old worn - out suit and shoes; __

I ain't got no cig - a - rettes. _ Ah, but
I don't pay no un - ion dues. _ I smoke

two hours of push - ing broom _ buys a
old sto - gies I have found, __

eight ___ by twelve four - bit room. _} I'm a
short ___ but not too big a - round. _}

man of

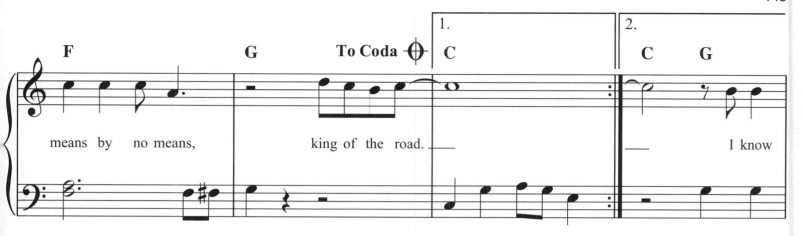

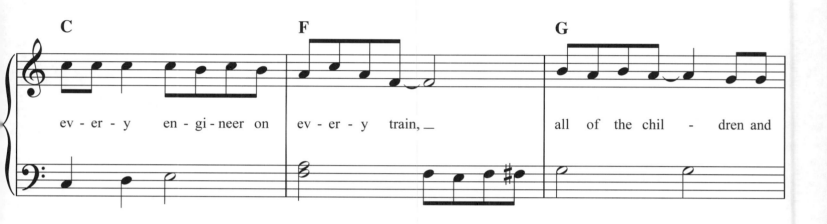

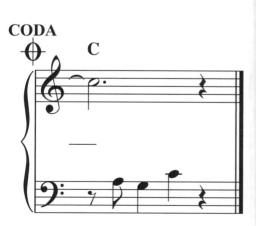

LOST IN THE FIFTIES TONIGHT
(In the Still of the Nite)

Words and Music by MIKE REID,
TROY SEALS and FRED PARRIS

Close your eyes ba - by,
(See additional lyrics)

fol - low my heart,

call on the mem-'ries

here in the dark. ___

We'll let the mag - ic

take us a - way. ___

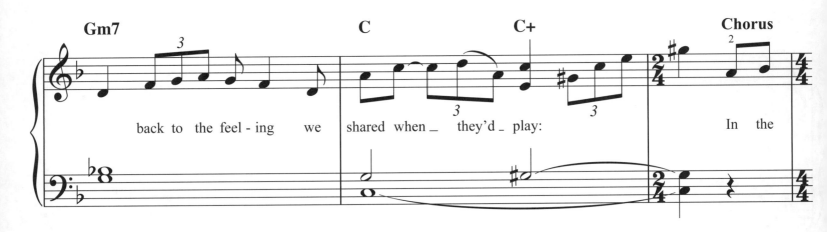

back to the feel - ing we

shared when ___ they'd ___ play:

In the

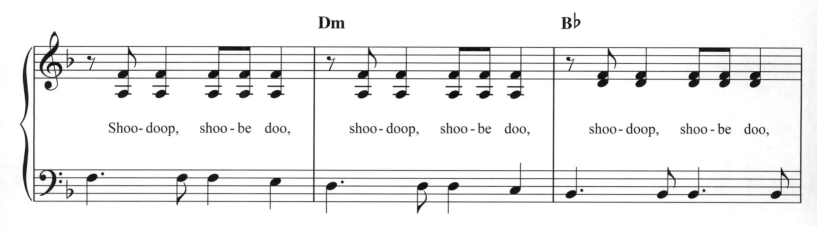

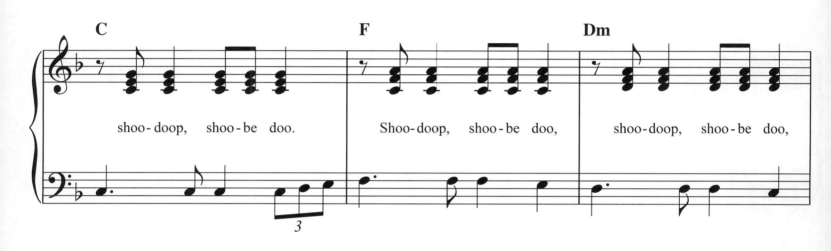

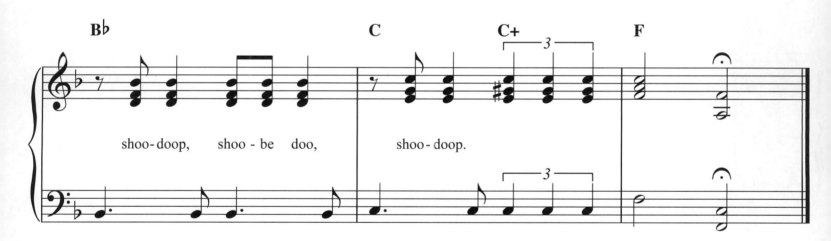

Additional Lyrics

These precious hours, we know can't survive.
Love's all that matters while the past is alive.
Now and for always, till time disappears,
We'll hold each other whenever we hear:
Chorus

LOVE WITHOUT END, AMEN

Words and Music by
AARON G. BARKER

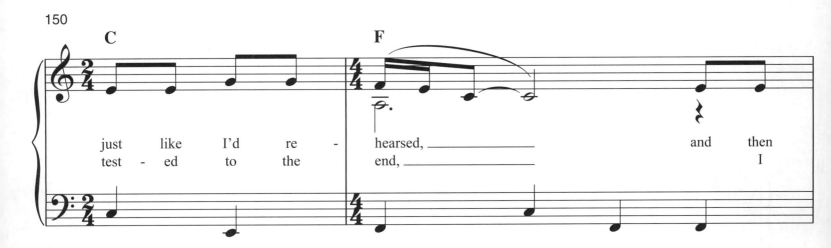

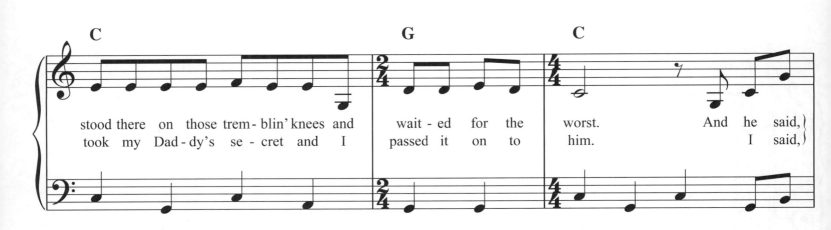

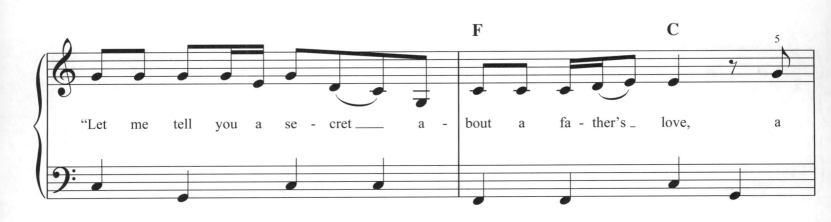

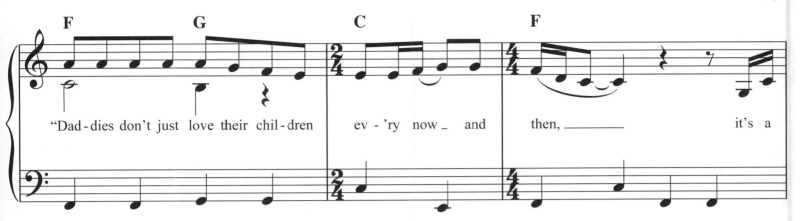

"Dad-dies don't just love their chil-dren ev-'ry now _ and then, _____ it's a

love with-out end, _ A - men." ___ It's a love with-out end, _ A - men. _

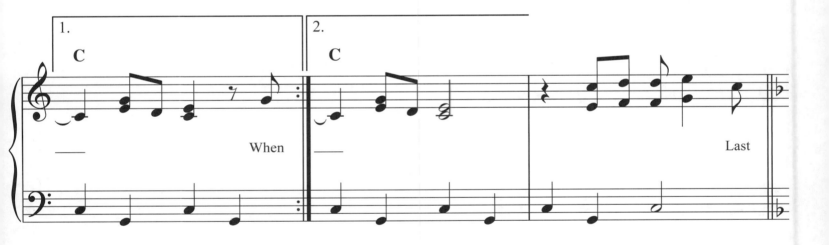

1.

When

2.

Last

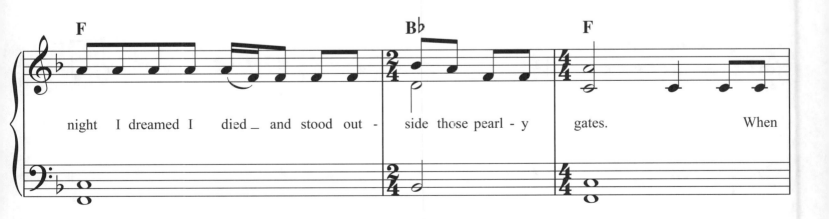

night I dreamed I died _ and stood out - side those pearl - y gates. When

sud - den - ly, I re - al - ized _ there must be some _ mis-take. If

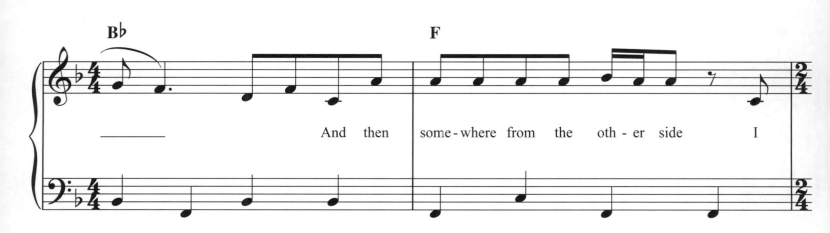

they know half the things _ I've done they'll _ nev - er let ___ me in. ___

___ And then some - where from the oth - er side I

heard these words a - gain. ___ And they said, "Let me tell you a se - cret ___ a-

bout a fa-ther's love,   a   se-cret that my dad-dy said was   just   be - tween _ us."

You see,   dad-dies don't just love their chil - dren   ev -'ry now _ and then, ____

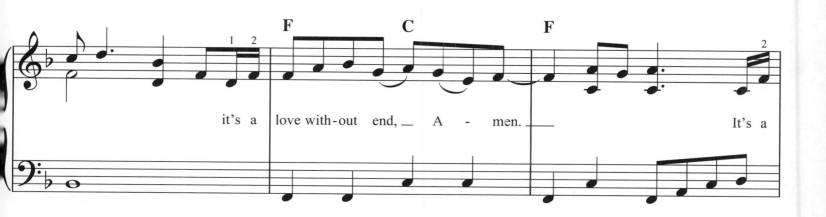

it's a love with-out end, _ A - men. ___   It's a

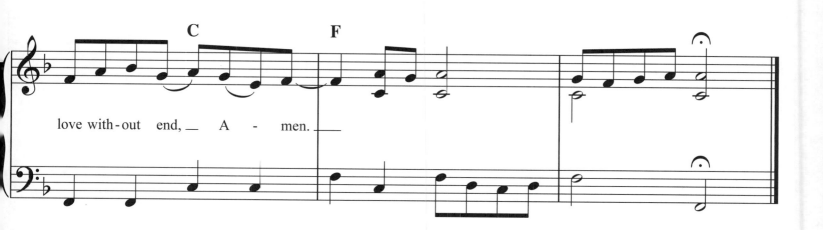

love with-out end, _ A - men. ___

MAMMAS DON'T LET YOUR BABIES GROW UP TO BE COWBOYS

Words and Music by ED BRUCE
and PATSY BRUCE

let 'em   pick   gui - tars   and   drive   them   old

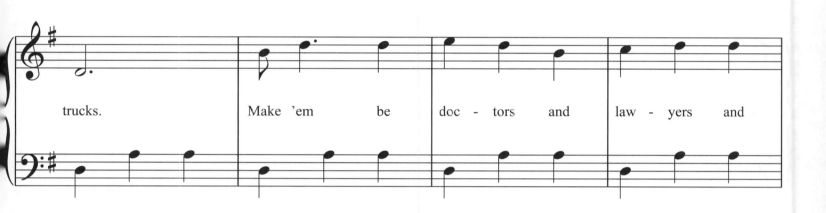

trucks.   Make 'em   be   doc - tors   and   law - yers   and

such.   Mam - mas, _____   don't   let   your

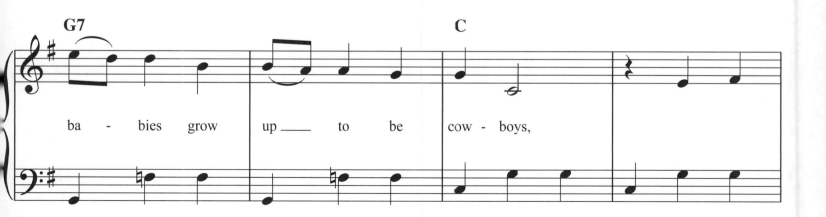

ba - bies   grow   up ___   to   be   cow - boys,

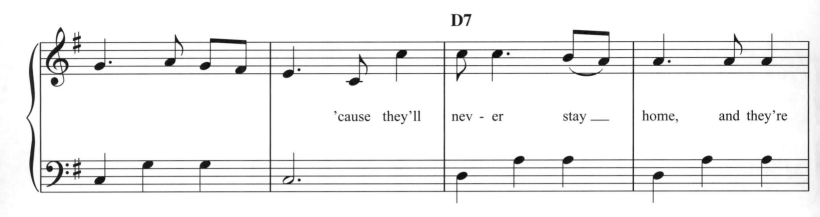

'cause they'll nev - er stay ___ home, and they're

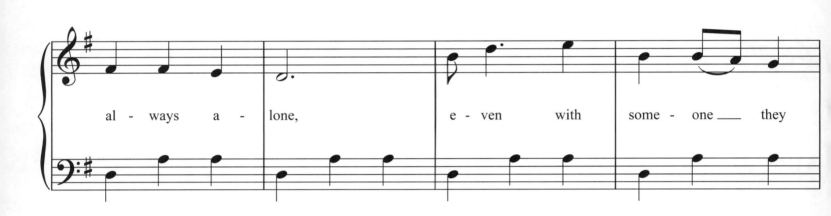

al - ways a - lone, e - ven with some - one ___ they

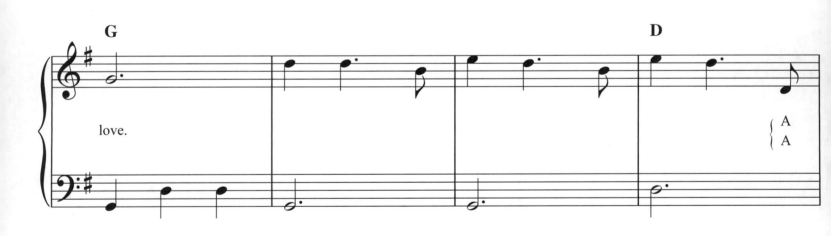

love.

{ A
{ A

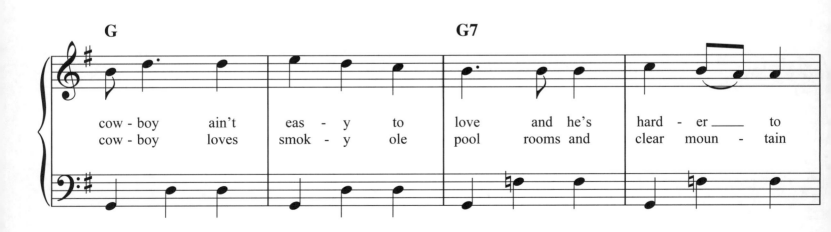

cow - boy ain't eas - y to love and he's hard - er ___ to
cow - boy loves smok - y ole pool rooms and clear moun - tain

157

C

hold.
morn - ings,

And it means

D7

more to him to give you a song than sil - ver or
lit - tle warm ___ pup - pies and chil - dren and girls of the

G   **D**

gold.
night.

G   **G7**

Bud - wei - ser buck - les and soft fad - ed Le - vis and
Them that don't know him won't like him and them that do

C

each night be - gins a new day.
some - times won't know how to take him.
He's not If you

D7

can't un - der - stand __ him __ and he don't die __ young, he'll
wrong, he's just dif - f'rent __ and his pride won't __ let him do

G

prob - a - bly just ride __ a - way.
things to make you think __ he's right.

1.
D

2.
D

G

LUCKENBACH, TEXAS
(Back to the Basics of Love)

Words and Music by BOBBY EMMONS
and CHIPS MOMAN

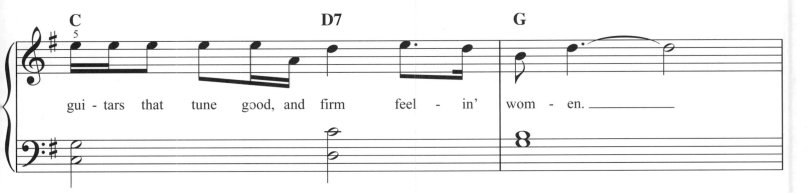

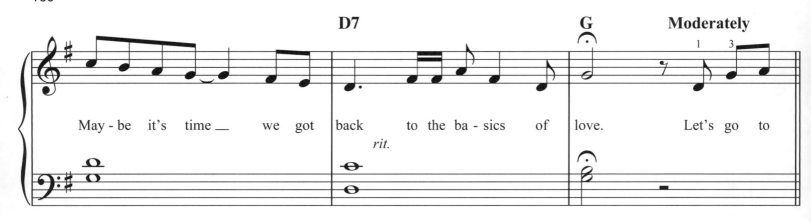

D7　　　　　　　　　　　**G**　　　**Moderately**

May - be it's time __ we got back to the ba - sics of love. Let's go to

rit.

Luck - en - bach, Tex - as with Way - lon and Wil - lie and the boys.

C

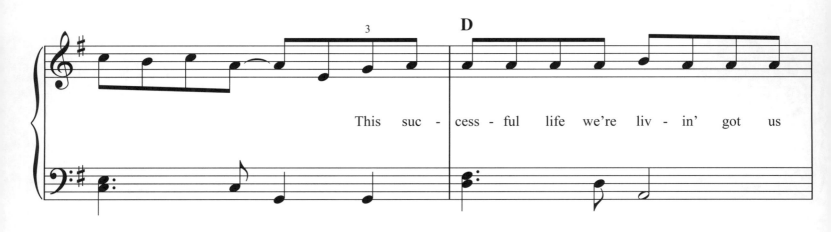

3　　　**D**

This suc - cess - ful life we're liv - in' got us

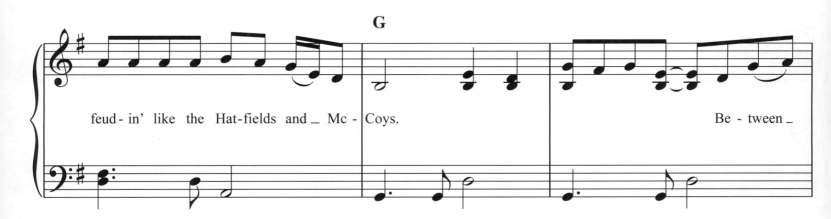

G

feud - in' like the Hat - fields and __ Mc - Coys.　　　Be - tween __

Hank Wil-liams' pain songs _ and New-ber-ry's train songs _ and "Blue Eyes Cry-in' in the

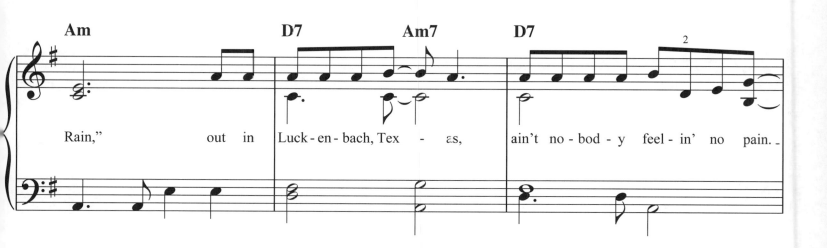

Rain," out in Luck-en-bach, Tex - as, ain't no-bod-y feel-in' no pain. _

To Coda

So, ba - by, let's sell your dia-mond ring,

buy some boots and fad - ed jeans and go ___ a - way. ___

This coat and tie is chok- in' me; in your high so - ci - e - ty you

cry ___ all day. We've been so bus - y keep- in'

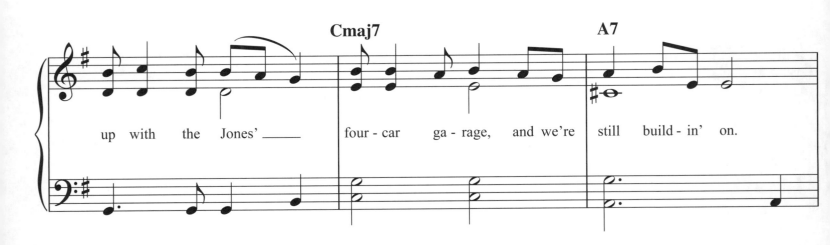

up with the Jones' ___ four - car ga - rage, and we're still build - in' on.

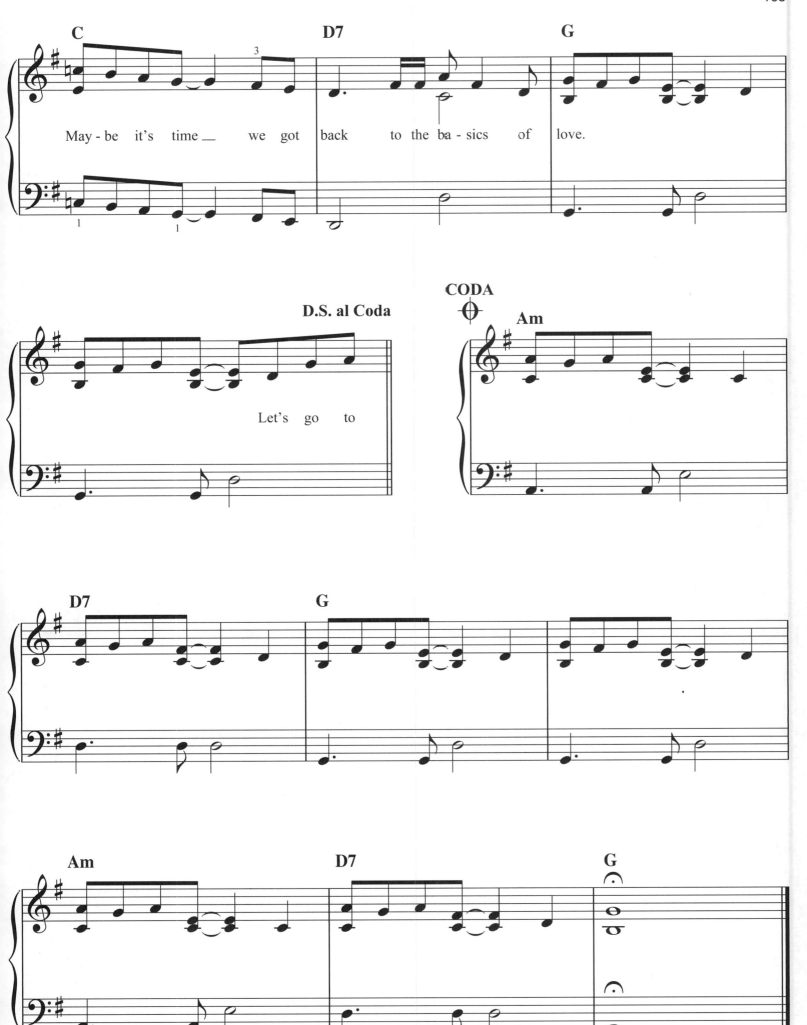

May - be it's time ___ we got back to the ba - sics of love.

D.S. al Coda

CODA

Let's go to

MAKE THE WORLD GO AWAY

Words and Music by
HANK COCHRAN

MY ELUSIVE DREAMS

Words and Music by CURLY PUTMAN
and BILLY SHERRILL

1. You fol-lowed me _____ to Tex - as, _____ you
2., 3. *(See additional lyrics)*

fol-lowed me _____ to U - tah, _____ we did - n't find it

there so we moved on. _____ You

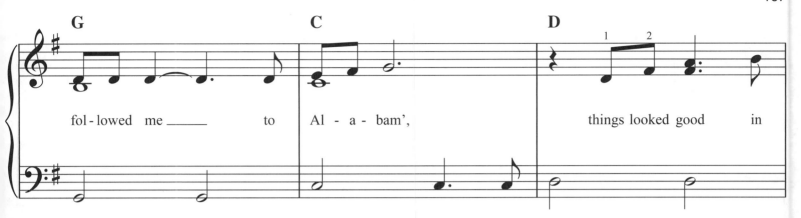

G fol-lowed me _____ to **C** Al - a - bam', **D** things looked good in

G Bir - ming - ham, we did - n't find it **C** there so we

D7 moved on. _____ I know you're tired of

Chorus **G**

C fol - low - ing **D7** my e - lu - sive dreams and _ schemes, **G**

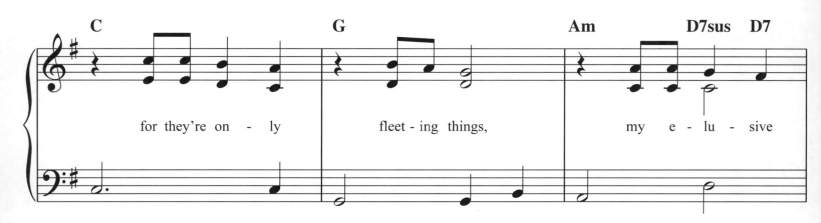

for they're on - ly   fleet - ing things,   my e - lu - sive

dreams.   You / And   dreams,

rit. my e - lu - sive dreams.

Additional Lyrics

2. You had my child in Memphis, I heard of work in Nashville,
   We didn't find it there so we moved on.
   To a small farm in Nebraska to a gold mine in Alaska,
   We didn't find it there so we moved on.
   Chorus

3. And now we've left Alaska because there was no gold mine,
   But this time only two of us moved on.
   Now all we have is each other and a little memory to cling to,
   And still you won't let me go on alone.
   Chorus

ROCKY TOP

Words and Music by BOUDLEAUX BRYANT
and FELICE BRYANT

Wish that I was on ol' Rock - y Top,
Once two strang - ers climbed ol' Rock - y Top,

down in the Ten - nes - see hills.
look - in' for a moon-shine still.

Ain't no smog - gy
Strang - ers ain't come

smoke from Rock - y Top,
down from Rock - y Top;

ain't no tel - e - phone bills.
reck - on they nev - er will.

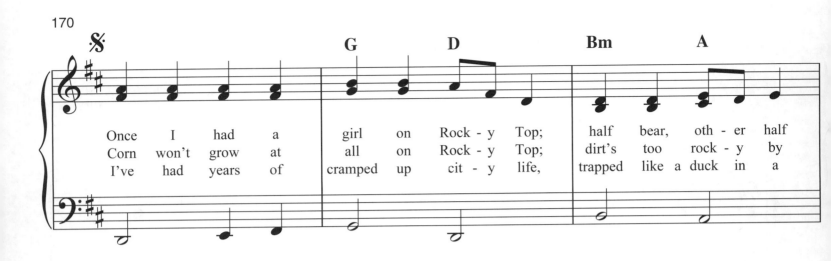

Once I had a | girl on Rock-y Top; | half bear, oth-er half
Corn won't grow at | all on Rock-y Top; | dirt's too rock-y by
I've had years of | cramped up cit-y life, | trapped like a duck in a

cat. | Wild as a mink, but | sweet as so-da pop;
far. | That's why ___ all the | folks on Rock-y Top
pen. | All I ___ know is | it's a pit-y life

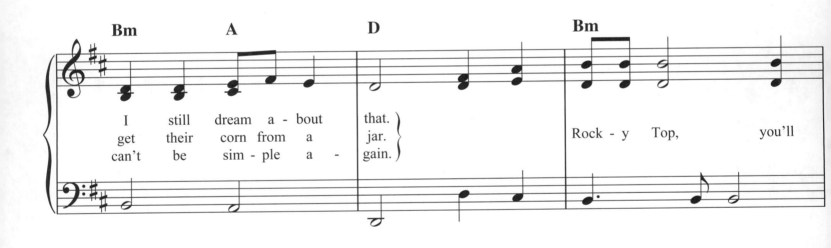

I still dream a-bout | that. | Rock-y Top, you'll
get their corn from a | jar. |
can't be sim-ple a-|gain. |

al - ways be | home, sweet home to | me.

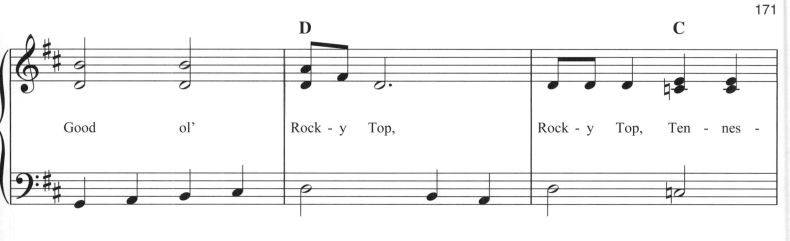

Good ol' Rock - y Top, Rock - y Top, Ten - nes -

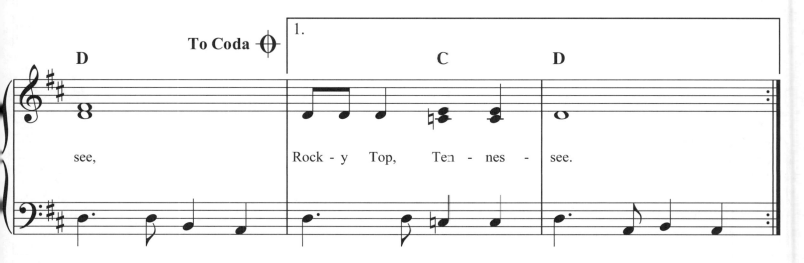

To Coda see, Rock - y Top, Ten - nes - see.

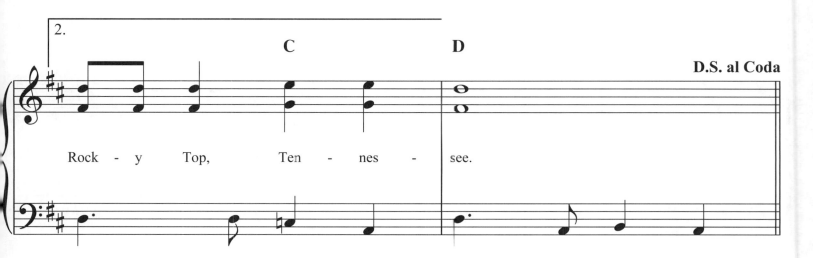

Rock - y Top, Ten - nes - see. **D.S. al Coda**

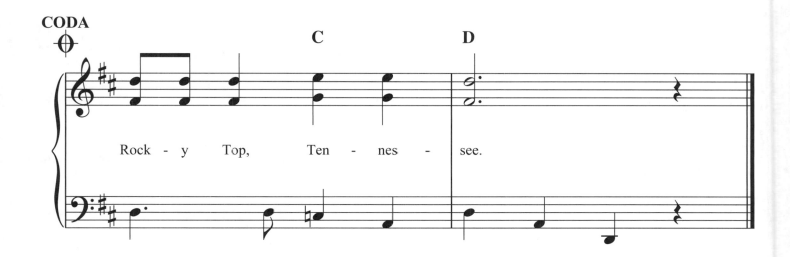

CODA Rock - y Top, Ten - nes - see.

NEED YOU NOW

Words and Music by HILLARY SCOTT,
CHARLES KELLEY, DAVE HAYWOOD
and JOSH KEAR

Moderately

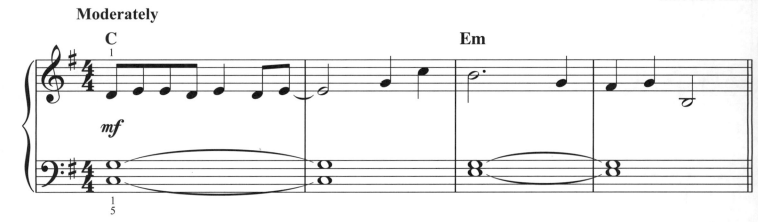

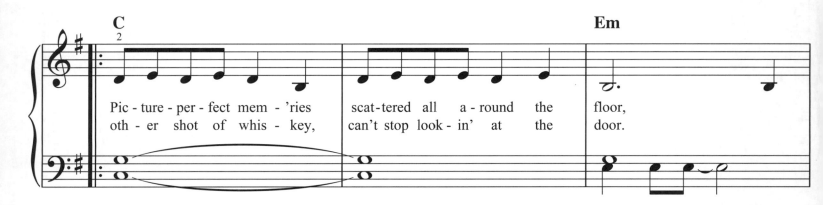

Pic - ture - per - fect mem - 'ries scat - tered all a - round the floor,
oth - er shot of whis - key, can't stop look - in' at the door.

reach - in' for the phone 'cause I can't fight it an - y -
Wish - in' you'd come sweep - in' in the way you did be -

more.}
fore.}

And I won - der if ___ I ev - er crossed ___ your

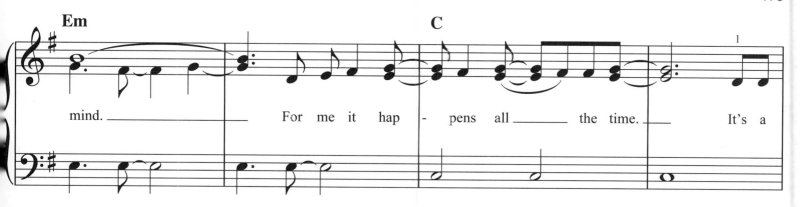

mind. _____ For me it hap - pens all _____ the time. _____ It's a

quar - ter af - ter one, I'm all a - lone and I need you now. _____
quar - ter af - ter one, I'm a lit - tle drunk and I need you now. _____
quar - ter af - ter one, I'm all a - lone and I need you now. _____

Said I would-n't call, but I lost all con - trol and I
Said I would-n't call, but I lost all con - trol and I
Said I would-n't call, but _____ I'm a lit - tle drunk

need you now. _____ And I don't know how _____ I can

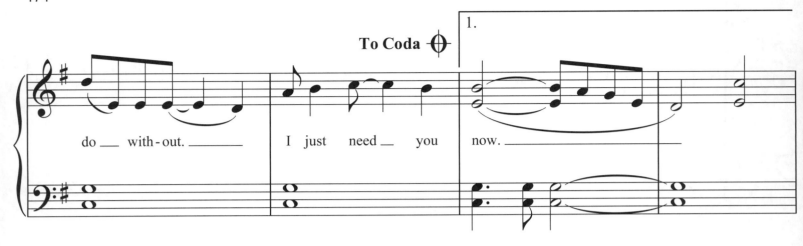

do — with-out. _____ I just need — you now. _____

An - now. _____ Guess I'd rath - er hurt __ than feel __

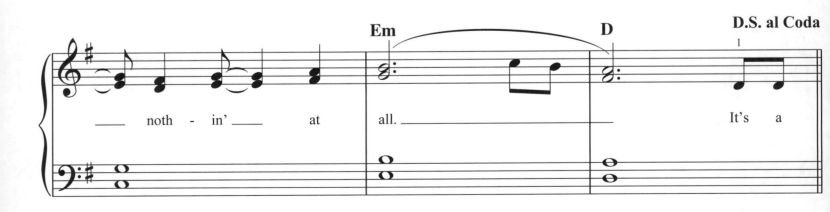

_____ noth - in' ____ at all. _____ It's a

RELEASE ME

Words and Music by ROBERT YOUNT,
EDDIE MILLER and DUB WILLIAMS

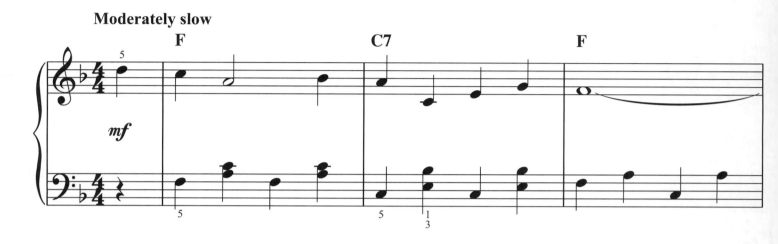

Please   re -   lease   me,   let   me
I   have   found   a   new   love,
Please   re -   lease   me,   can't   you

go, _____   for   I   don't
dear, _____   and   I   will
see _____   you'd   be   a

RHINESTONE COWBOY

Words and Music by
LARRY WEISS

With a steady beat

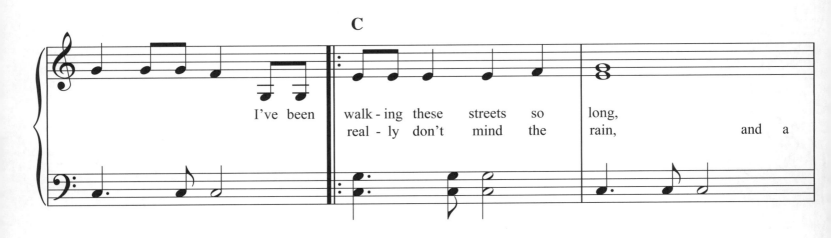

I've been walk-ing these streets so long,
real-ly don't mind the rain, and a

sing-in' the same old song, I know ev-'ry crack in these
smile can hide the pain, but you're down when you're rid-ing a

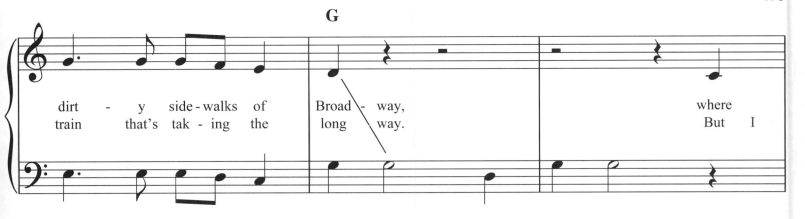

dirt - y side-walks of Broad-way, where
train that's tak-ing the long way. But I

hus - tle is the name of the game and
dream of the things the I'll do with a

nice guys get washed a - way like the snow in the rain.
sub - way to - ken and a dol - lar in - side __ my shoe.

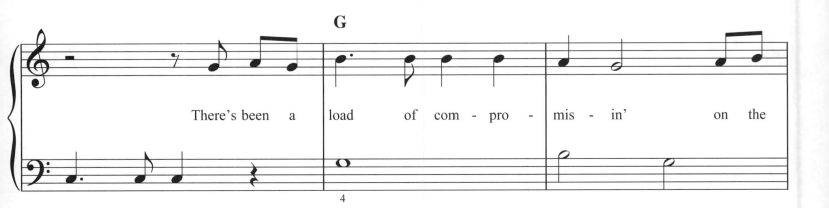

There's been a load of com - pro - mis - in' on the

4

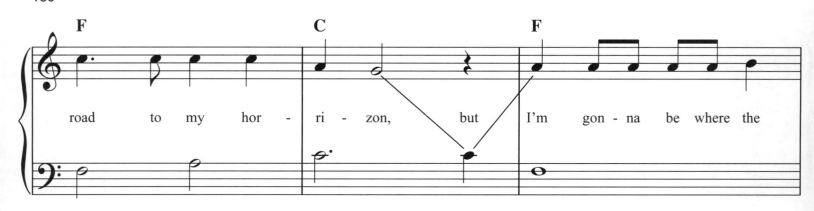

road to my hor - ri - zon, but I'm gon - na be where the

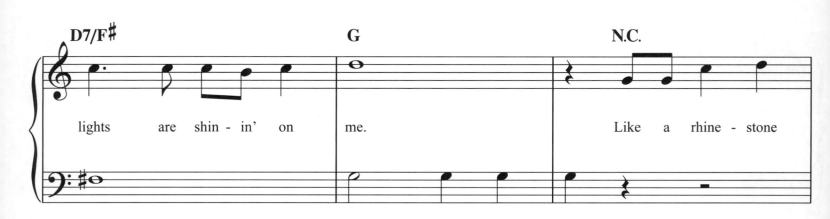

lights are shin - in' on me. Like a rhine - stone

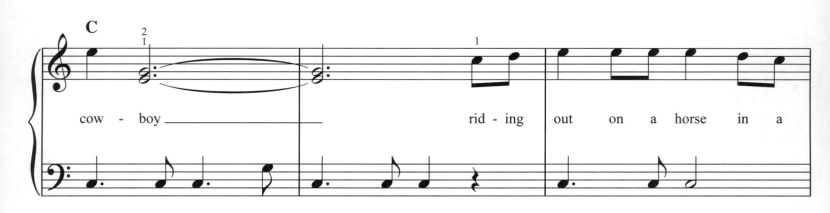

cow - boy _____ rid - ing out on a horse in a

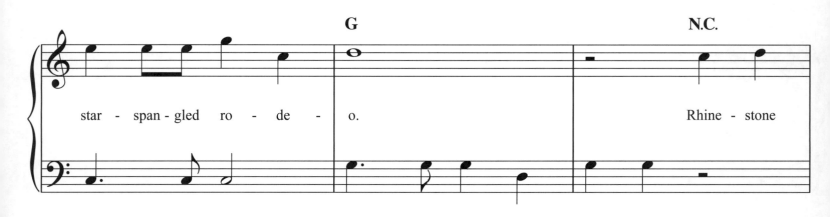

star - span - gled ro - de - o. Rhine - stone

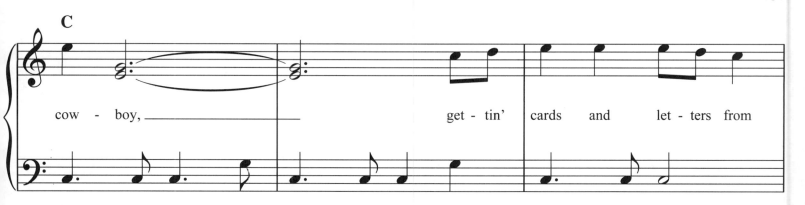

cow - boy, _____ get - tin' cards and let - ters from

peo - ple I don't e - ven know and of - fers com - ing o - ver the

phone.

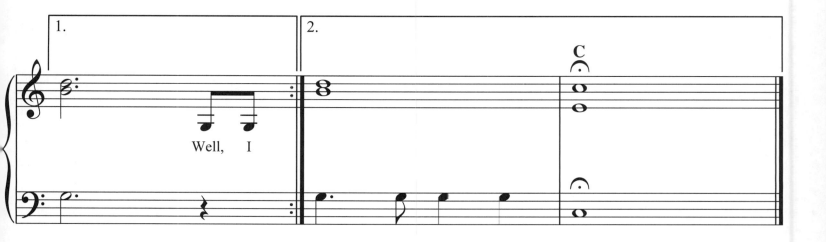

1.

2.

Well, I

RING OF FIRE

Words and Music by MERLE KILGORE
and JUNE CARTER

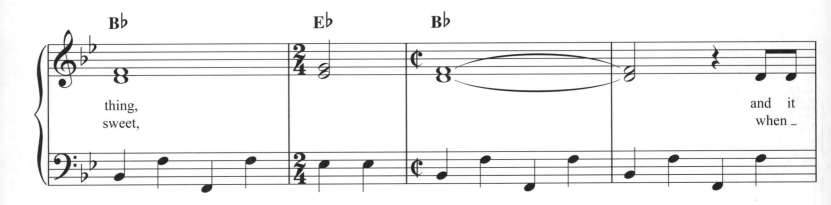

makes _____ a fi - ery ring.
hearts _____ like ours ____ beat.

Bound _____ by wild de -
I fell for you like a

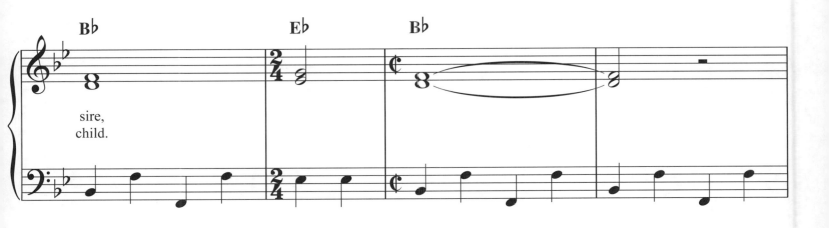

sire,
child.

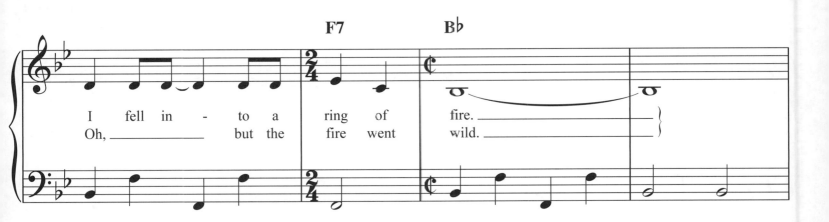

I fell in - to a ring of fire. _____
Oh, _____ but the fire went wild. _____

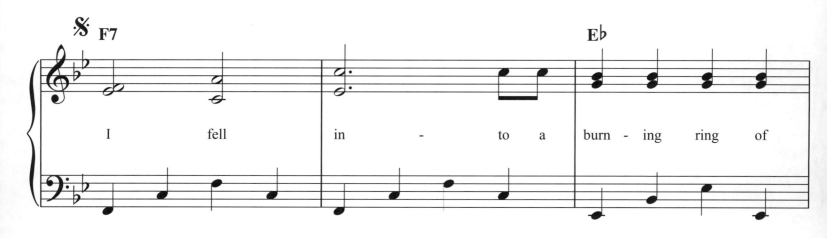

I fell in - to a burn - ing ring of

fire. _____ I went down, down, down and the

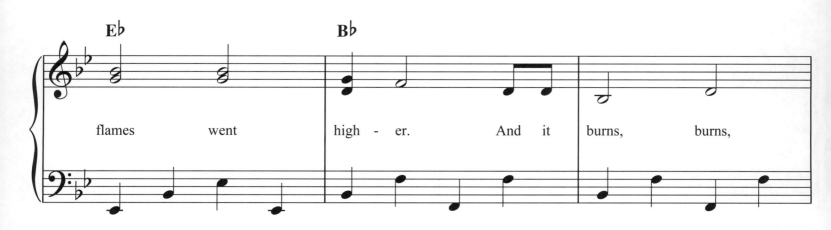

flames went high - er. And it burns, burns,

To Coda ⊕

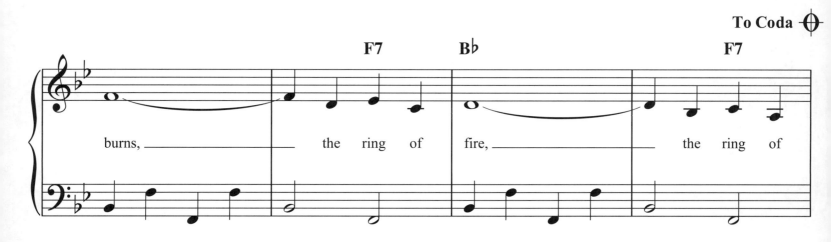

burns, _____ the ring of fire, _____ the ring of

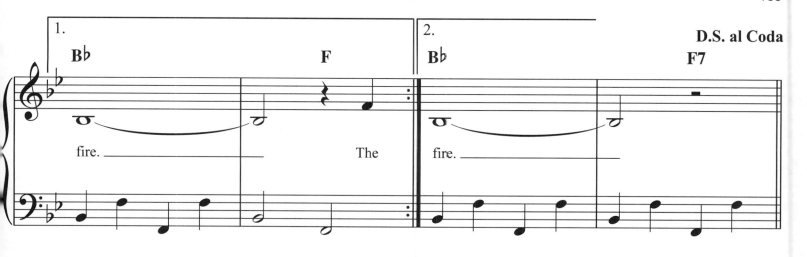

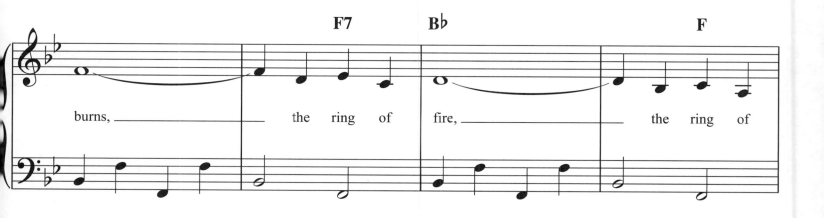

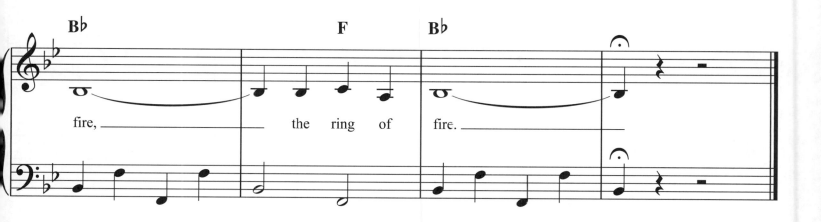

RUBY, DON'T TAKE YOUR LOVE TO TOWN

Words and Music by
MEL TILLIS

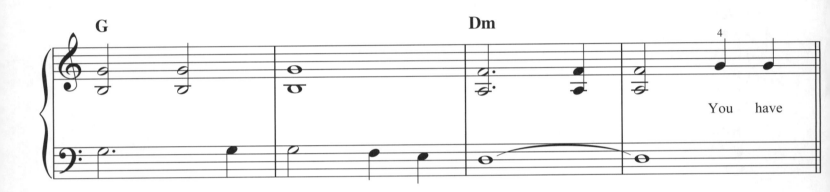

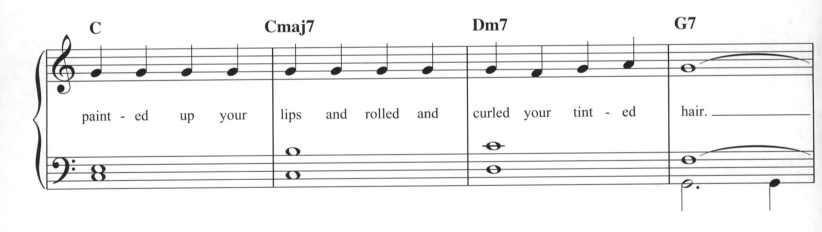

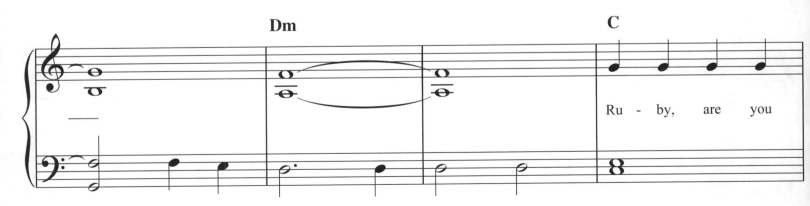

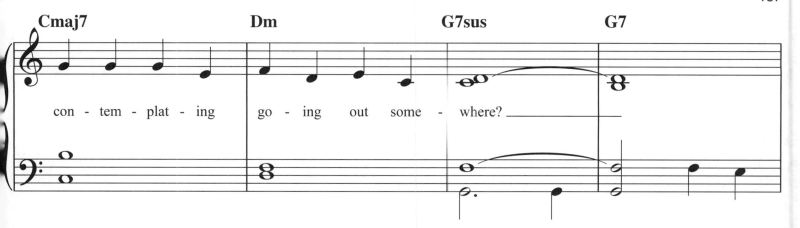

con - tem - plat - ing go - ing out some - where? ___

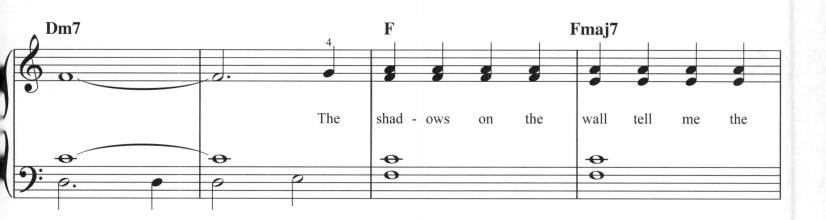

The shad - ows on the wall tell me the

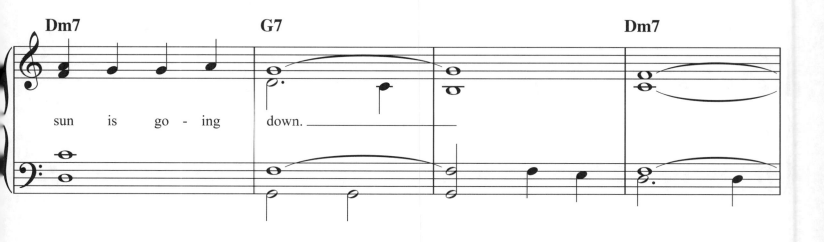

sun is go - ing down. ___

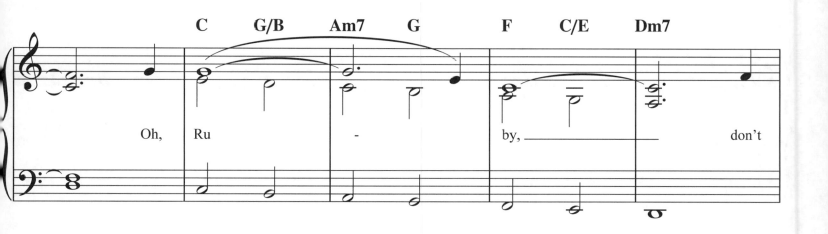

Oh, Ru - by, ___ don't

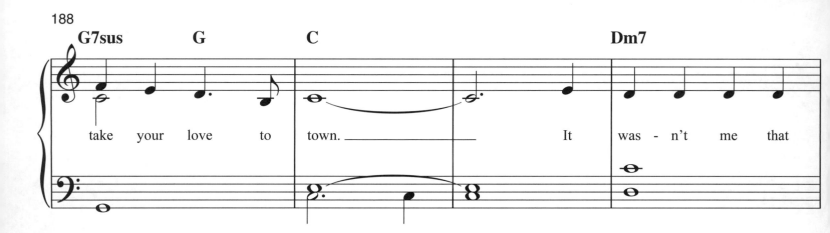

take your love to town. It was-n't me that

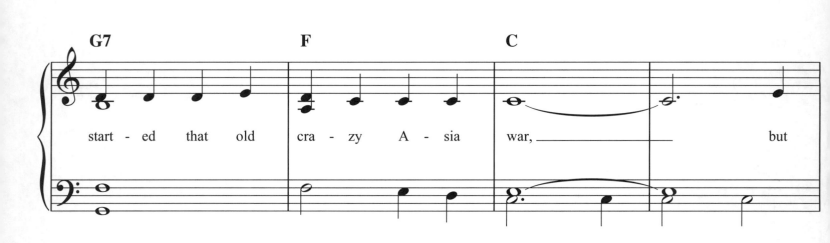

start - ed that old cra - zy A - sia war, but

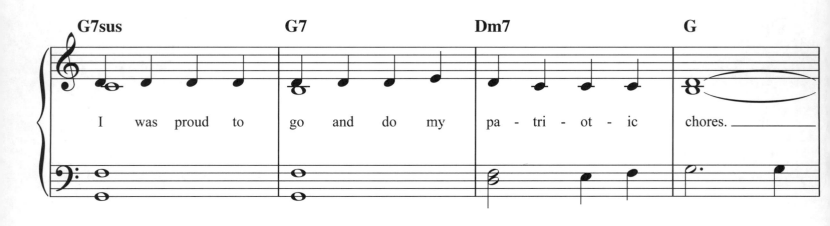

I was proud to go and do my pa - tri - ot - ic chores.

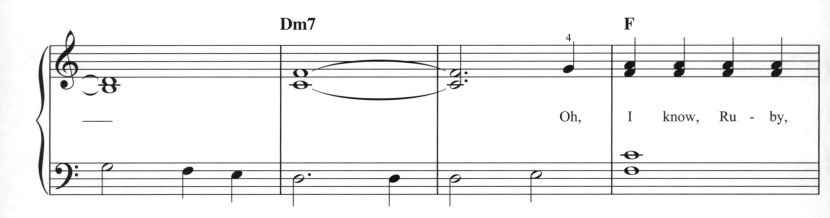

Oh, I know, Ru - by,

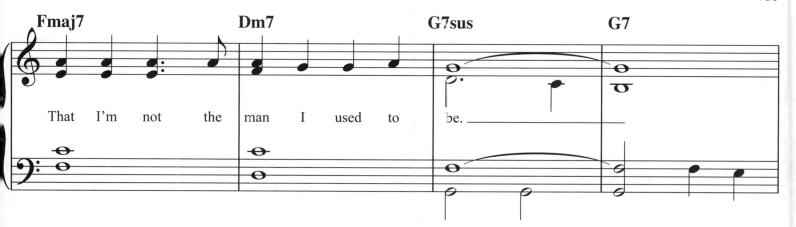

That I'm not the man I used to be.____

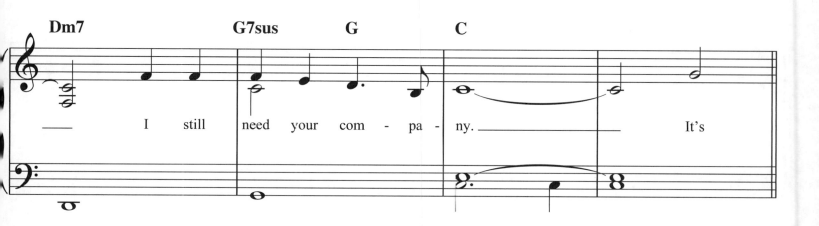

But, Ru - by,_____

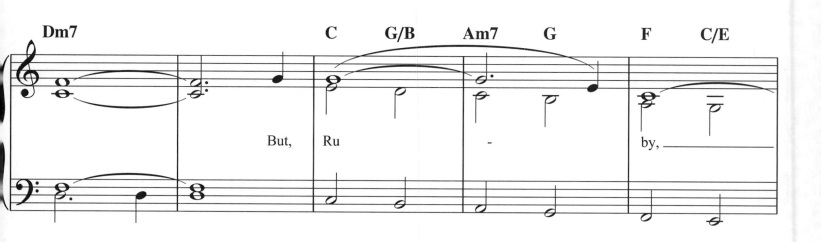

____ I still need your com - pa - ny._____ It's

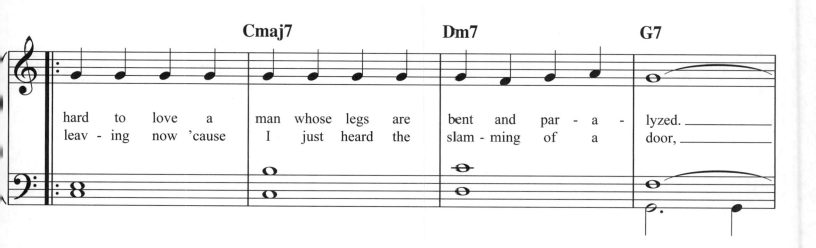

hard to love a man whose legs are bent and par - a - lyzed.____
leav - ing now 'cause I just heard the slam - ming of a door,____

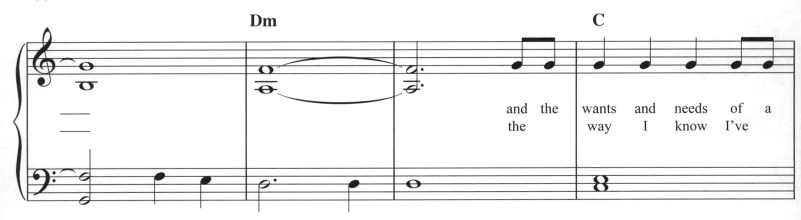

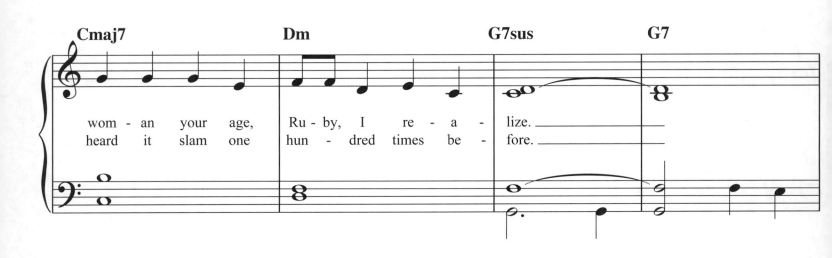

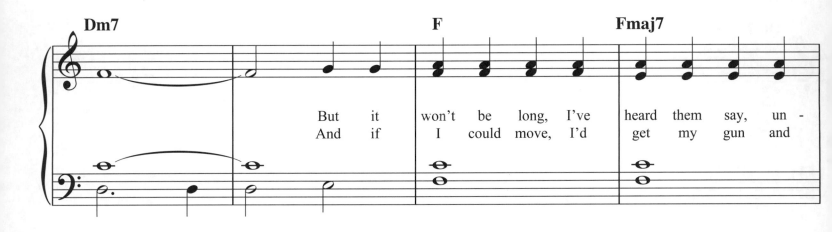

A SATISFIED MIND

Words and Music by JOE "RED" HAYES
and JACK RHODES

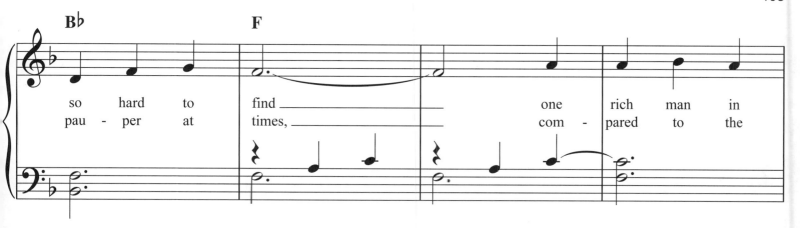

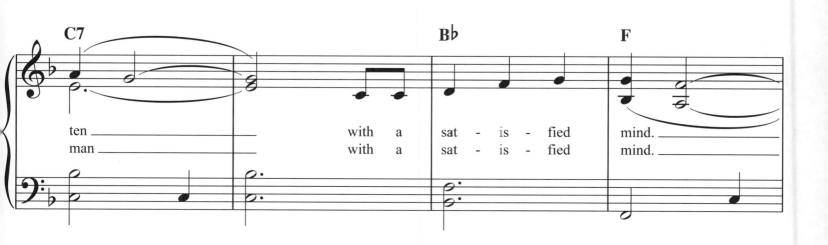

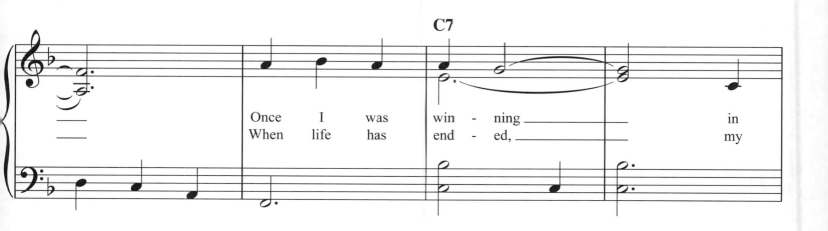

SIXTEEN TONS

Words and Music by
MERLE TRAVIS

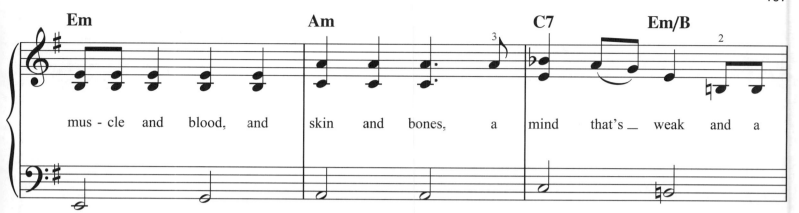

muscle and blood, and skin and bones, a mind that's _ weak and a

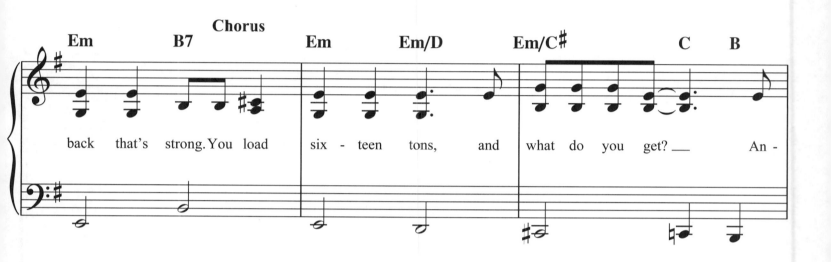

Chorus

back that's strong. You load six - teen tons, and what do you get? __ An -

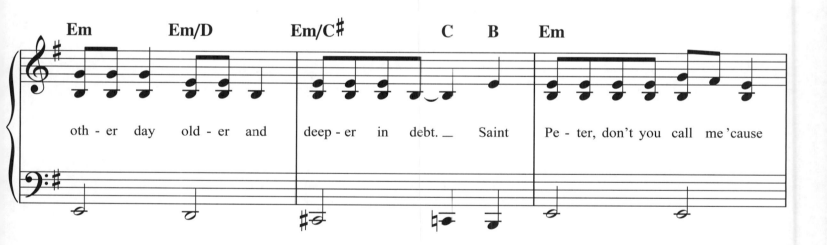

oth - er day old - er and deep - er in debt. __ Saint Pe - ter, don't you call me 'cause

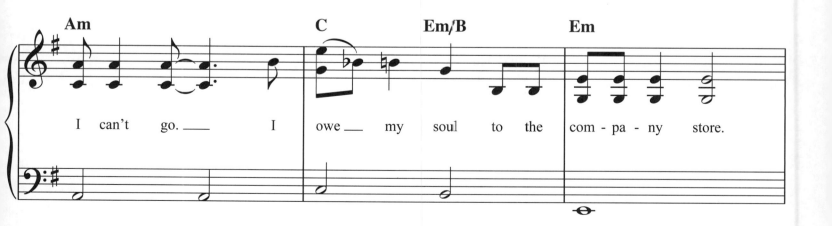

I can't go. __ I owe __ my soul to the com - pa - ny store.

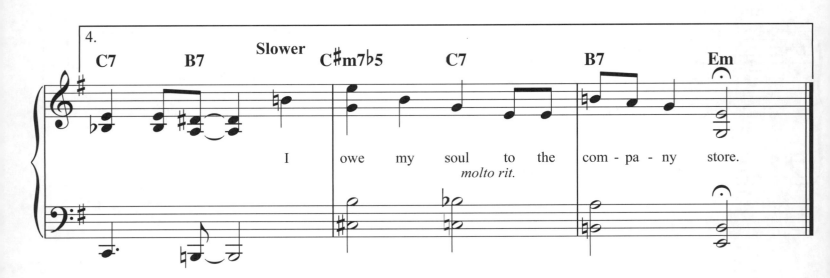

Additional Lyrics

2. I was born one mornin' when the sun didn't shine.
   I picked up my shovel and I walked to the mine.
   I loaded sixteen tons of number nine coal
   And the straw boss said, "Well - a bless my soul."
   Chorus

3. I was born one mornin', it was drizzling rain.
   Fightin' and trouble are my middle name.
   I was raised in a cane brake by an ole mama lion,
   Cain't no high toned woman make me walk the line.
   Chorus

4. If you see me comin', better step aside.
   A lotta men didn't; a lotta men died.
   One fist of iron, the other of steel,
   If the right one don't a-get you, then the left one will.
   Chorus

STAND BY ME

Words and Music by JERRY LEIBER,
MIKE STOLLER and BEN E. KING

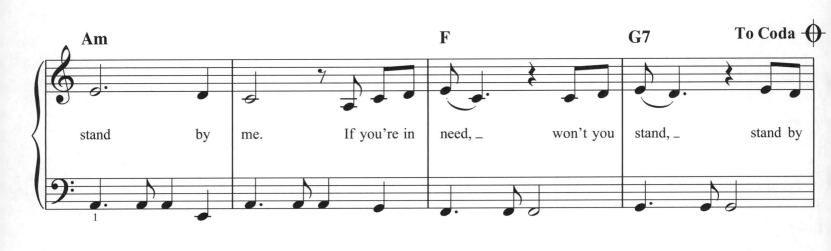

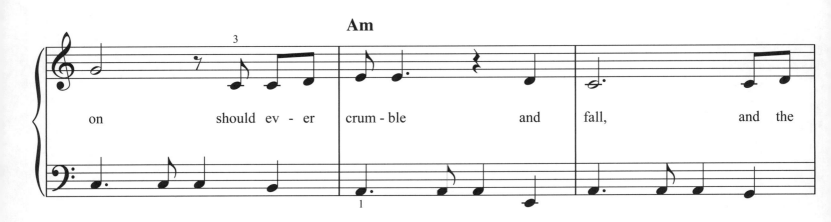

F   G7   C

moun - tains _____ should fall ___ to the sea, _____

Am

no, I won't _ be a - fraid, _ no, I won't ___ shed a

F   G7   C

tear just as long _ as you stand, _ stand by me.

D.S. al Coda

Dar - ling, stand _____ by

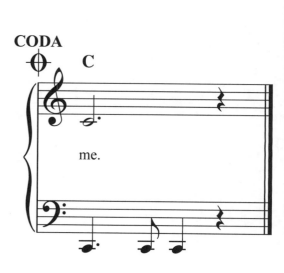

CODA

C

me.

SMOKY MOUNTAIN RAIN

Words and Music by KYE FLEMING
and DENNIS MORGAN

her name. ____ Smok-y Moun-tain rain, ___

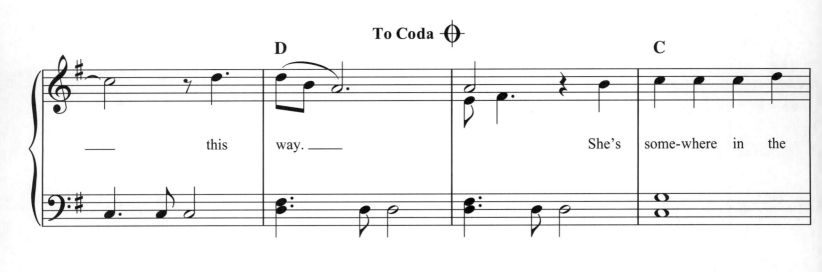

____ I'll keep on search - ing; I can't go on hurt - ing ____

To Coda ⊕

____ this way. ____ She's some-where in the

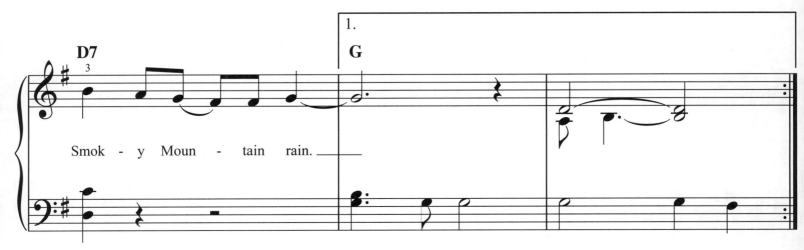

Smok - y Moun - tain rain. ___

I can't blame her for let-ting go,

a wom-an needs some-one warm ___ to hold. ___ I feel the rain run-ning

down ___ my face; ___ I'll find her no mat-ter what ___ it takes.

D.S. al Coda

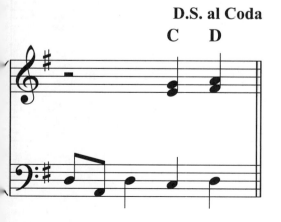

CODA

STAND BY YOUR MAN

Words and Music by TAMMY WYNETTE
and BILLY SHERRILL

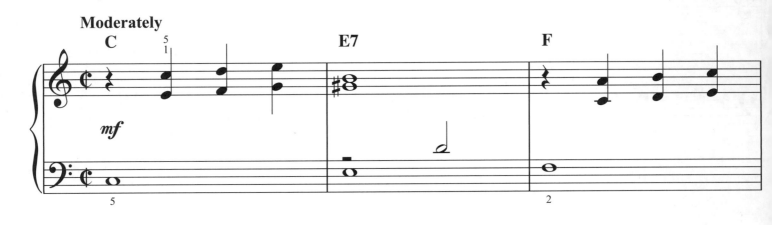

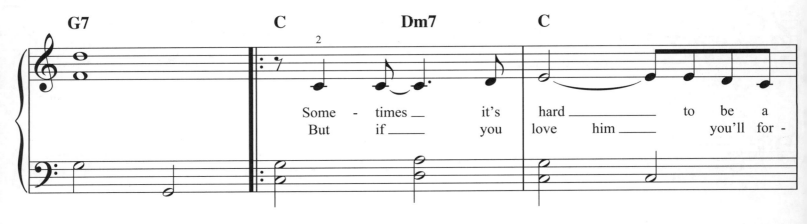

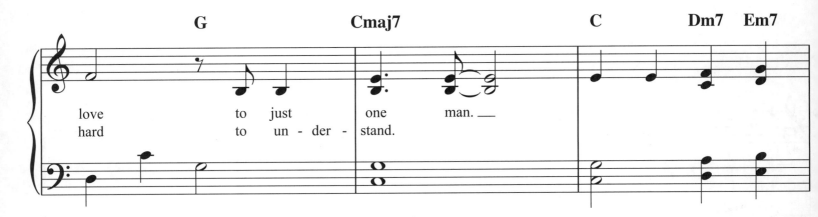

You'll have ___ bad times
And if you love him,

and he'll have

good times, ___

do - in' things that you don't ___ un - der-

stand. ___

oh, ___ be proud of

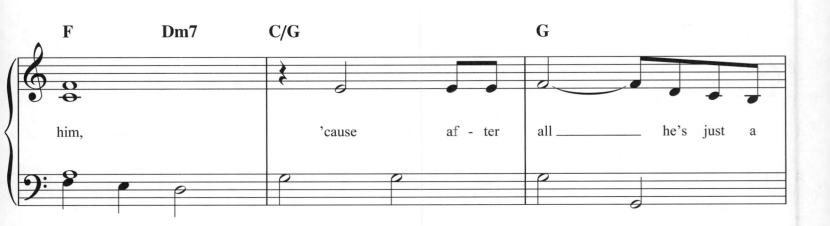

him,

'cause af - ter all ___ he's just a

C   F   C   % C

man. _____

Stand by your

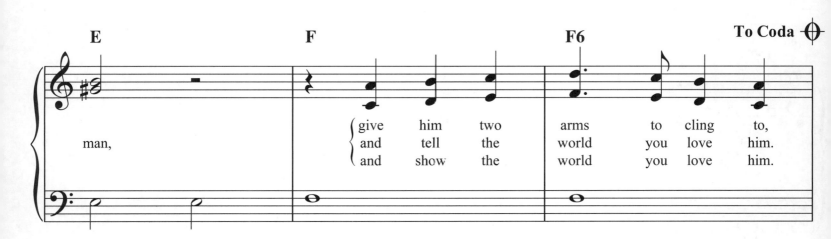

E   F   F6   **To Coda**

man,

give   him   two   arms   to   cling   to,
and   tell   the   world   you   love   him.
and   show   the   world   you   love   him.

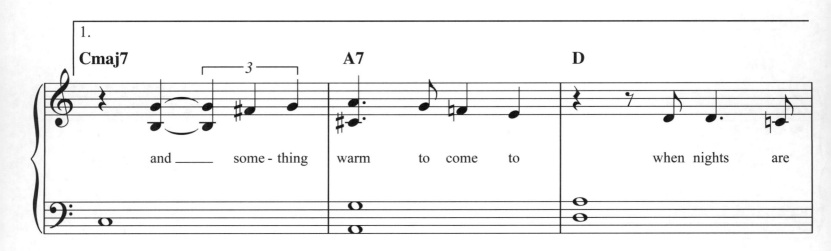

1.
Cmaj7   A7   D

and ____ some - thing   warm   to   come   to   when   nights   are

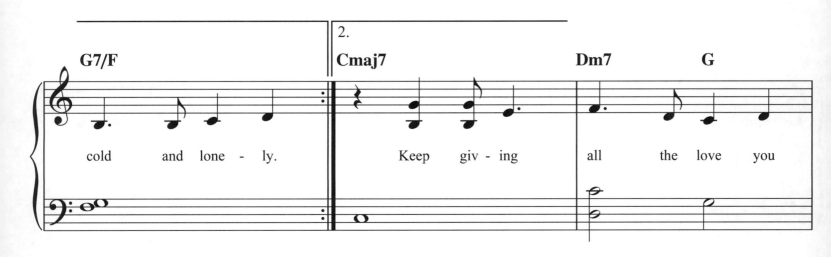

G7/F   2.
       Cmaj7   Dm7   G

cold   and   lone - ly.   Keep   giv - ing   all   the   love   you

209

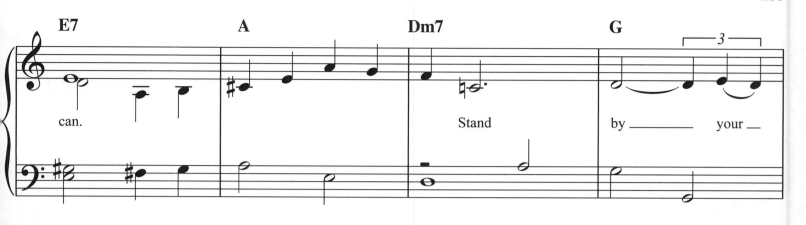

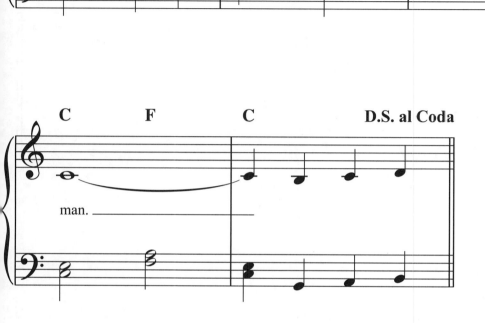

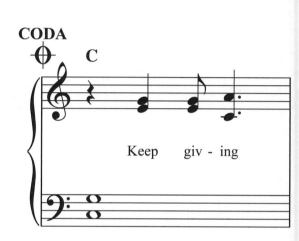

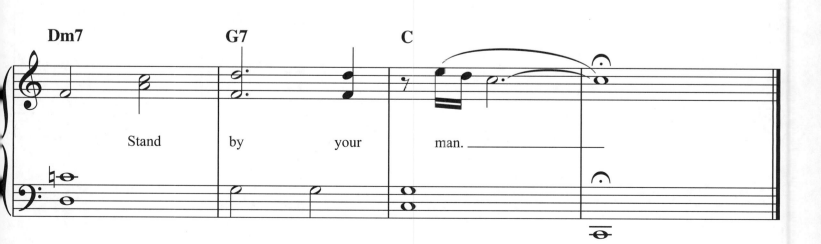

SWEET DREAMS

Words and Music by
DON GIBSON

can't I for - get you and start my life a -
can't I for - get the past, and start lov - ing some - one

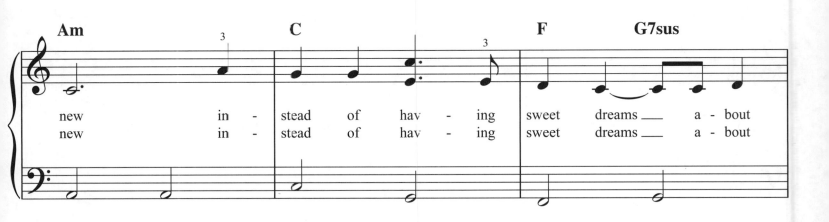

new in - stead of hav - ing sweet dreams ___ a - bout
new in - stead of hav - ing sweet dreams ___ a - bout

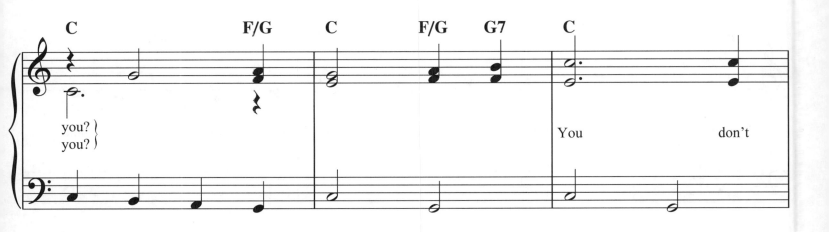

you?
you?

You don't

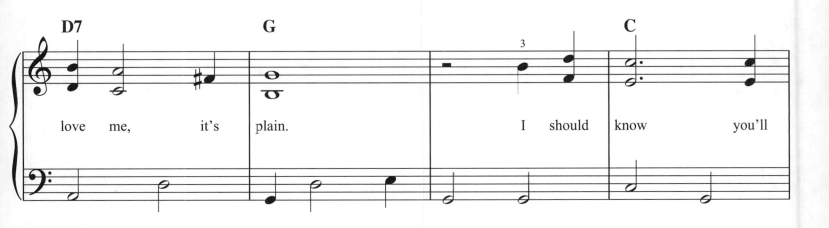

love me, it's plain. I should know you'll

212

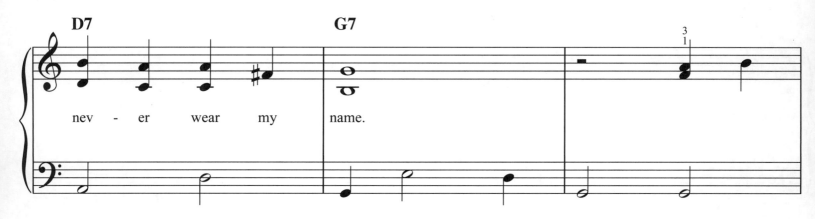

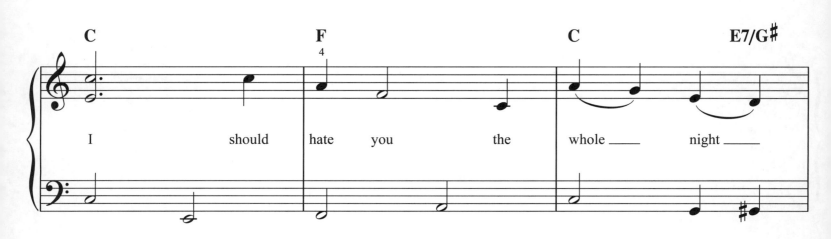

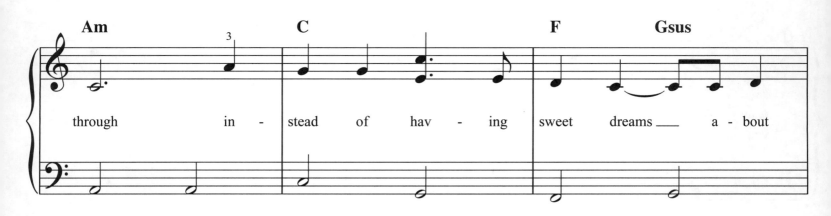

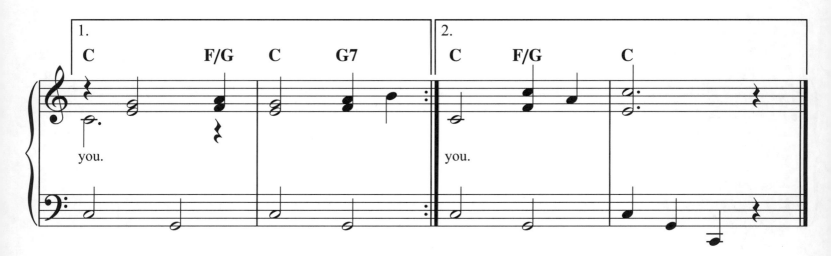

TENNESSEE WALTZ

Words and Music by REDD STEWART
and PEE WEE KING

Country Waltz

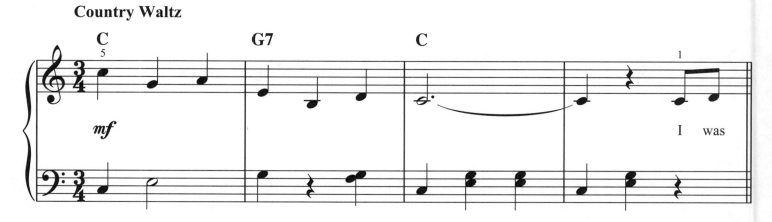

see. _____ In - tro - duced him _____ to my

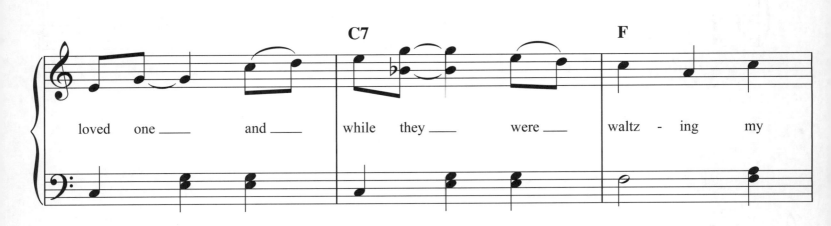

loved one _____ and _____ while they _____ were _____ waltz - ing my

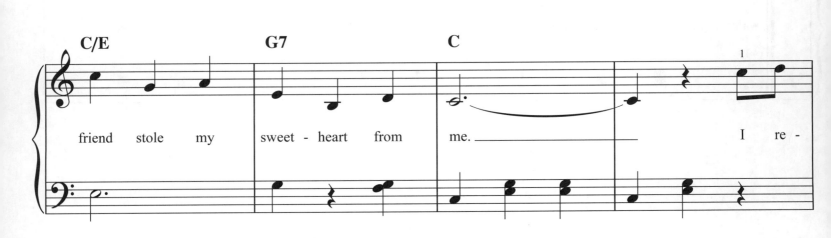

friend stole my sweet - heart from me. _____ I re -

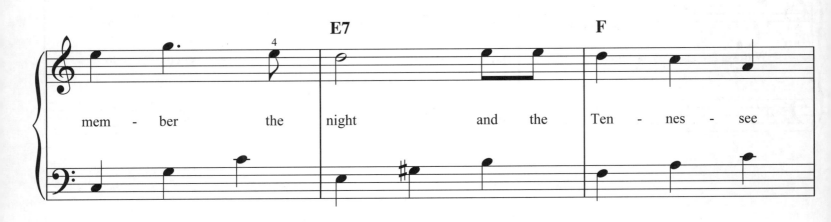

mem - ber the night and the Ten - nes - see

215

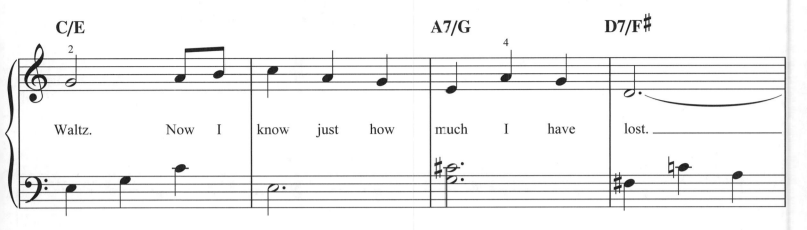

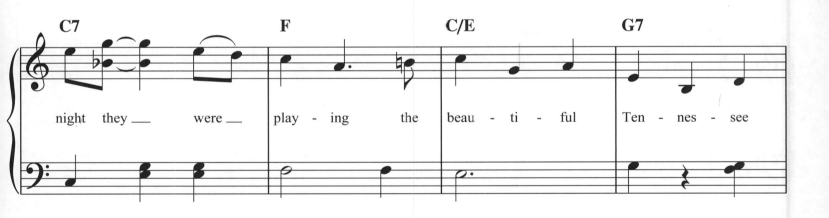

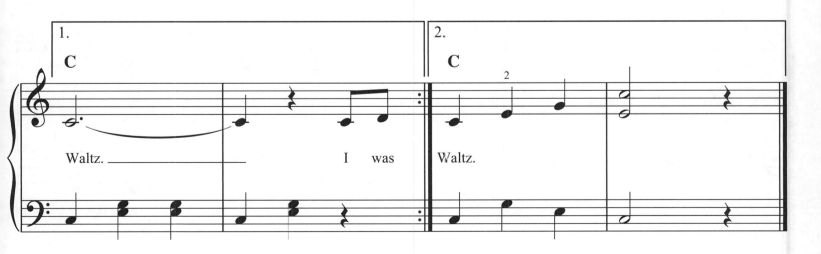

WABASH CANNONBALL

Words and Music by
A.P. CARTER

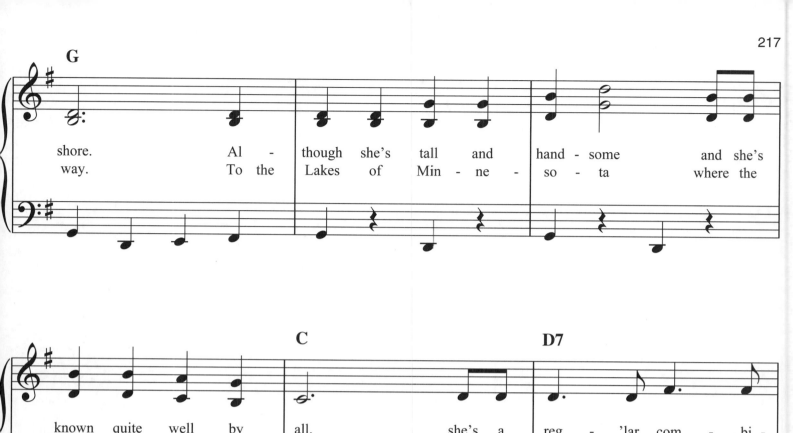

shore. Al -
way. To the

though she's tall and
Lakes of Min - ne -

hand - some
so - ta

and she's
where the

known quite well by
rip - pling wa - ters

all,
fall,

she's a
no

reg - 'lar com - bi -
chang - es can be

1.
G

na - tion
tak - en

of the
on the

Wa - bash Can - non -
Wa - bash Can - non -

ball.

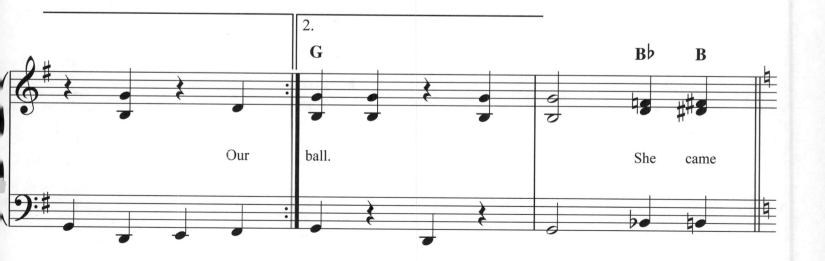

2.
G

Our

ball.

B♭   **B**

She came

217

C

down from Bir - ming - ham   one   cold De - cem - ber
lis - ten to the   jin - gle   and the rum - ble and the

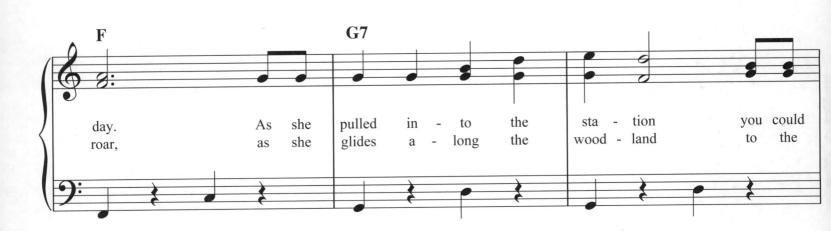

F   **G7**

day.   As she pulled in - to the sta - tion   you could
roar,   as she glides a - long the wood - land   to the

C

hear all the peo - ple say: There's a gal from Ten - nes -
hills and ___ to the shore.   Hear the might - y rush of the

F

see,   she is long and she is tall.   She
en - gine hear the lone - some ho - boes call,   while she's

G7

come from Bir - ming - ham _____ on the Wa - bash Can - non -
trav - 'ling through the jun - gle on the Wa - bash Can - non -

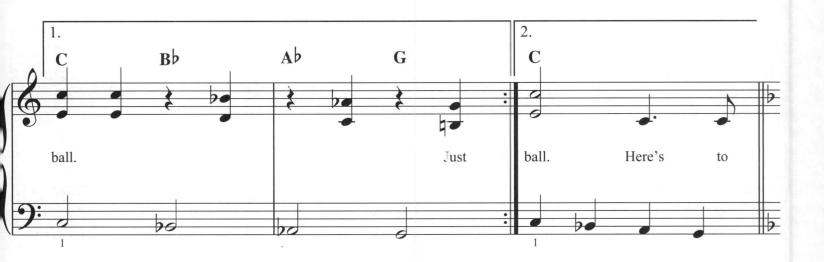

1.
C **B♭** **A♭** **G** 2. **C**

ball. Just ball. Here's to

F

old man Dad - dy Clax - ton may his name for - ev - er

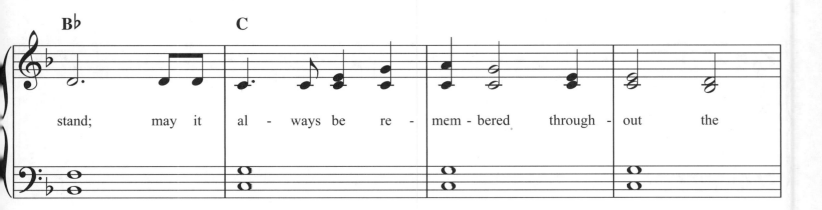

B♭ **C**

stand; may it al - ways be re - mem - bered through - out the

F

land. His earth - ly race is o - ver and the

cur - tains 'round him fall. **Bb** We'll **C** car - ry him home to

vic - t'ry on the Wa - **Bb** bash **Eb/G** Can - **E** non -

F ball. **Bb7** **F** **Gb7b5** **F**

8vb

THANK GOD I'M A COUNTRY BOY

Words and Music by
JOHN MARTIN SOMMERS

G   C   G

sim - ple kind of life nev - er did me no harm, rais - in' me a fam - i - ly and

F   D   G   C

work - in' on a farm. My days are all filled with an eas - y coun-try charm: ___ Thank

G   D   G   D

God I'm a coun-try boy. ___ Well, I got me a fine wife, I

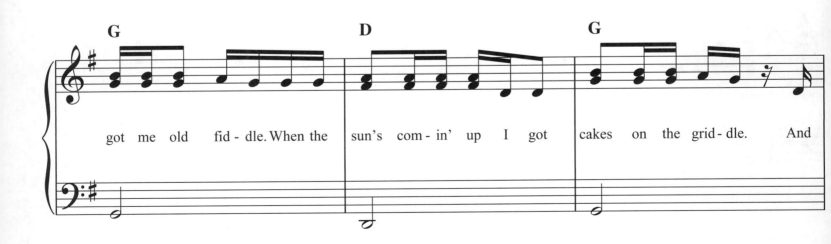

G   D   G

got me old fid - dle. When the sun's com - in' up I got cakes on the grid - dle. And

Additional Lyrics

2. When the work's all done and the sun's settin' low, I pull out my fiddle and I rosin up the bow.
   But the kids are asleep so I keep it kind-a low: Thank God I'm a country boy.
   I'd play "Sally Goodin" all day if I could, but the Lord and my wife wouldn't take it very good.
   So I fiddle when I can and I work when I should: Thank God I'm a country boy.

3. I wouldn't trade my life for diamonds or jewels, I never was one of them money-hungry fools.
   I'd rather have my fiddle and my farmin' tools: Thank God I'm a country boy.
   Yeah, city folk drivin' in a black limousine, a lotta sad people thinkin' that's mighty keen.
   Well, folks, let me tell you now exactly what I mean: I thank God I'm a country boy.

4. Well, my fiddle was my daddy's till the day he died, and he took me by the hand and held me close to his side.
   He said, "Live a good life and play my fiddle with pride, and thank God you're a country boy."
   My daddy taught me young how to hunt and how to whittle; he taught me how to work and play a tune on the fiddle.
   He taught me how to love and how to give just a little: Thank God I'm a country boy.

THROUGH THE YEARS

Words and Music by STEVE DORFF
and MARTY PANZER

Tenderly, in 2

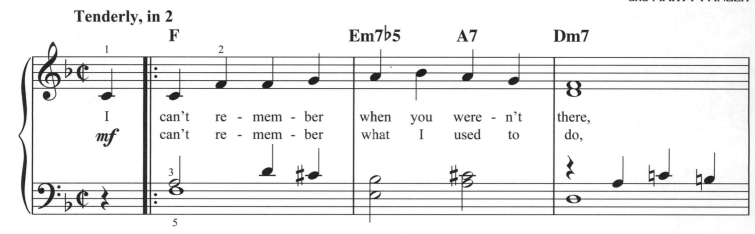

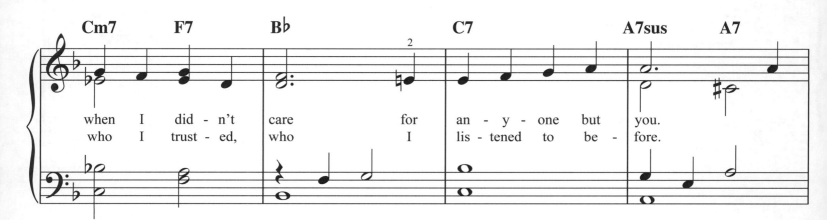

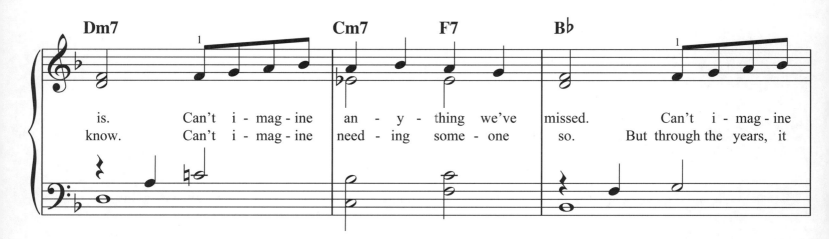

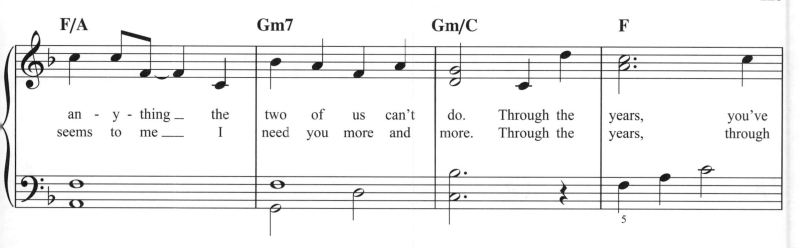

an - y - thing __ the two of us can't do. Through the years, you've
seems to me __ I need you more and more. Through the years, through

nev - er let me down, you've turned my life a - round. The
all the good and bad, I knew how much I had. I've

sweet - est days I've found, I've found with you. Through __ the years, I've
al - ways been so glad to be with you. Through __ the years, it's

nev - er been a - fraid, I've loved the life we've made. And
bet - ter ev - 'ry day. You've kissed my tears a - way. As

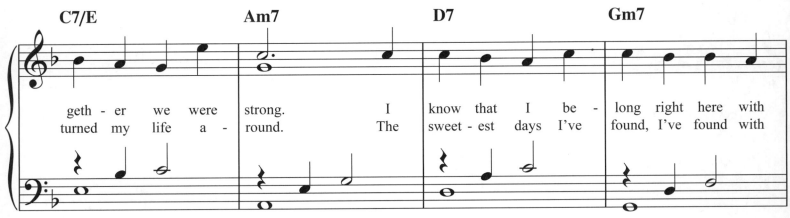

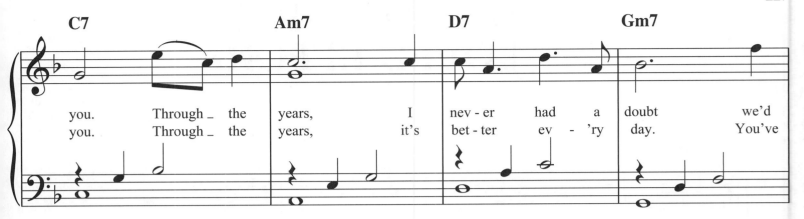

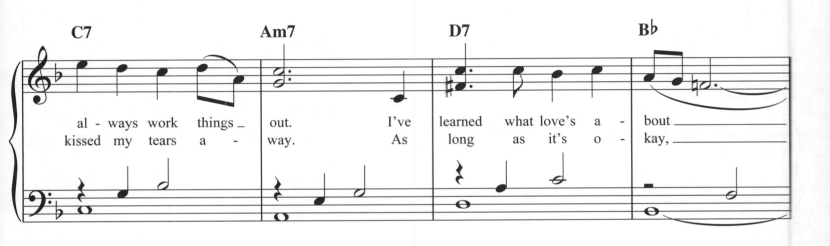

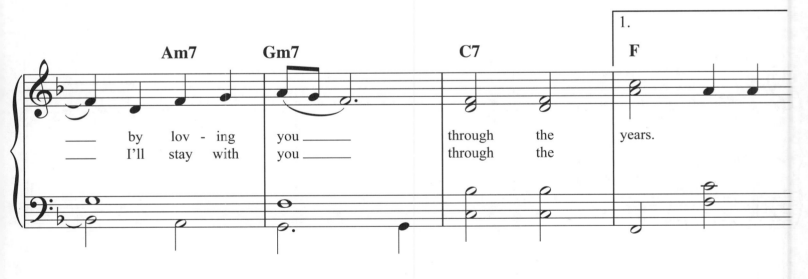

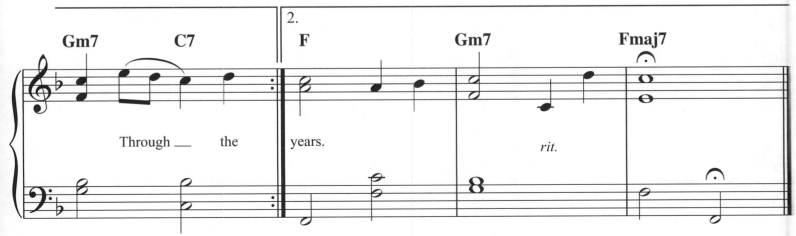

TO ALL THE GIRLS I'VE LOVED BEFORE

Words by HAL DAVID
Music by ALBERT HAMMOND

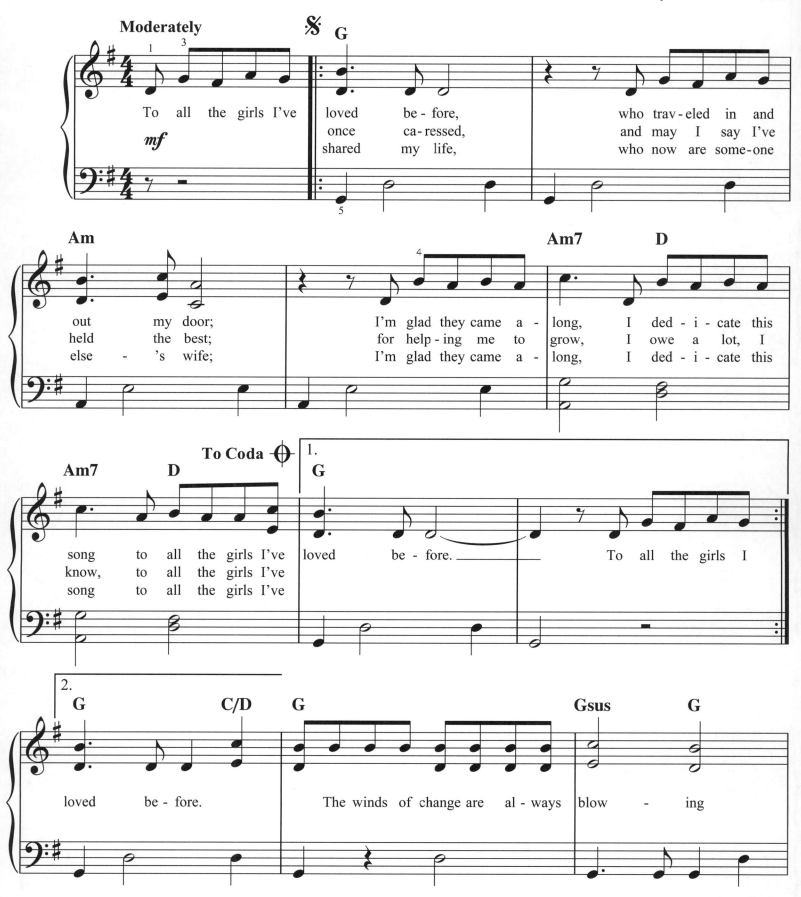

and ev-'ry time I tried to stay, the winds of change con-tin-ued

blow - ing, and they just car-ried me a - way.

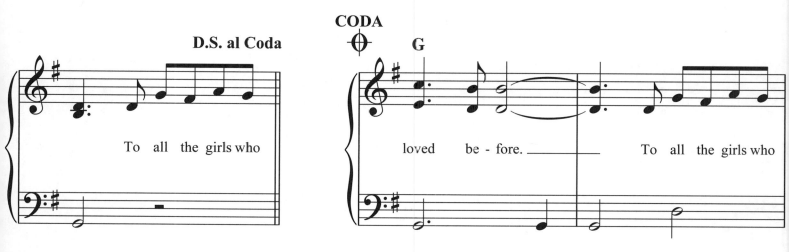

D.S. al Coda

CODA

To all the girls who loved be-fore. To all the girls who

cared for me; who filled my nights with ec - sta - sy,

they live with-in my heart, I'll al-ways be a part of all the girls I've

loved be-fore. The winds of change are al-ways blow - ing

and ev-'ry time I tried to stay, the winds of change con-tin-ued

blow - ing, and they just car-ried me a-way.

WALKIN' AFTER MIDNIGHT

Lyrics by DON HECHT
Music by ALAN W. BLOCK

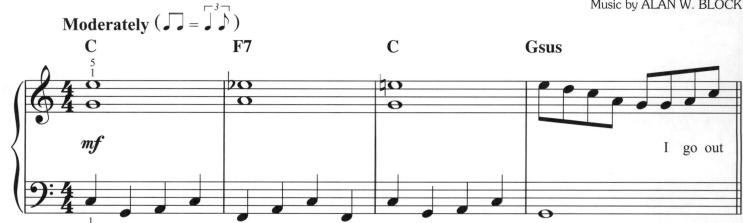

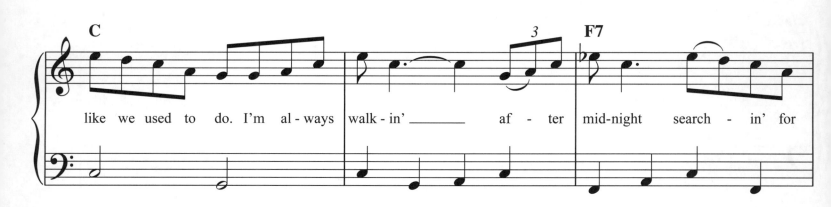

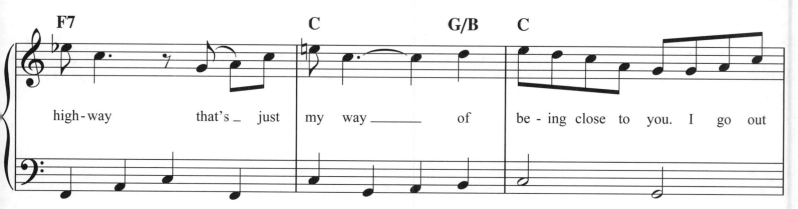

high-way   that's just | my way _____ of | be - ing close to you. I go out

walk - in' __   af - ter | mid - night search - in' for | you.

I stop to | see a weep - in' wil - low | cry - in' on his pil - low,

may - be he's cry - in' for | me.   And | as the sky turns gloom - y,

night winds whis-per to me. I'm lone - ly as lone - ly as can be. I'll go out

walk - in' _____ af - ter mid - night _____ in ___ the star - light _____ and

pray that you may be some-where just walk - in' _____ af - ter mid - night search - in' for

1.

2.

me. _____

I go out me.

WALKING IN THE SUNSHINE

Words and Music by
ROGER MILLER

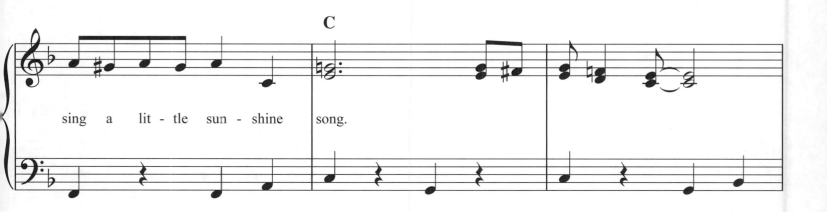

236

Think a-bout a good time had a long time a-go; ___

B♭ **B♭7**

think a-bout for-get-ting 'bout your wor-ries and ___ your woes. ___

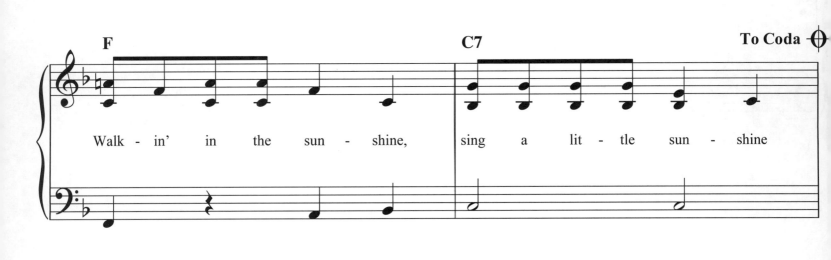

F **C7** **To Coda**

Walk-in' in the sun-shine, sing a lit-tle sun-shine

F **F7**

song.

La la ___ la la la dee oh, wheth - er the weath - er be

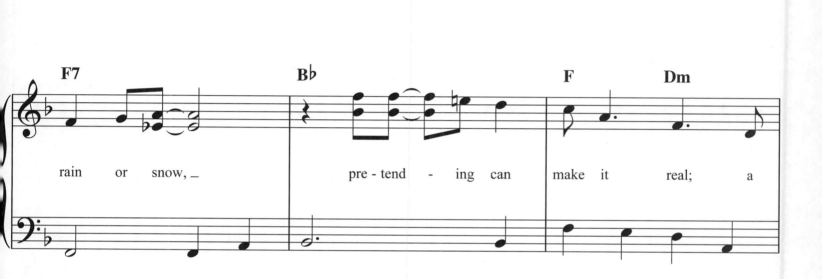

rain or snow, ___ pre - tend - ing can make it real; a

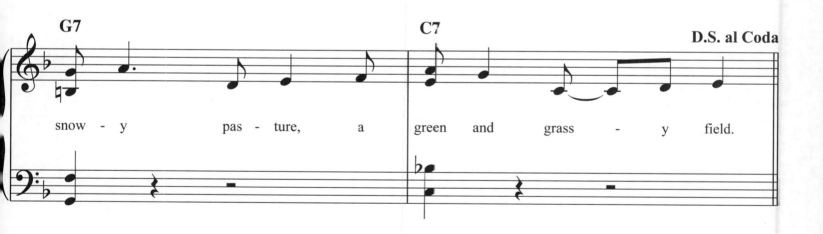

D.S. al Coda

snow - y pas - ture, a green and grass - y field.

CODA

song.

WALKING THE FLOOR OVER YOU

Words and Music by
ERNEST TUBB

Bright Texas Swing

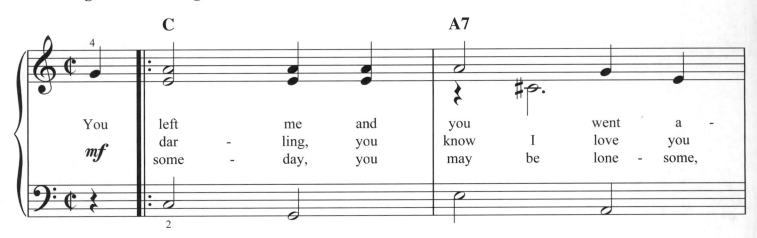

You left me and you went a-
dar - ling, and you know I love you
some - day, you may be lone - some,

way,
well,
too,

you
said that you'd be
love you more than
walk - ing the

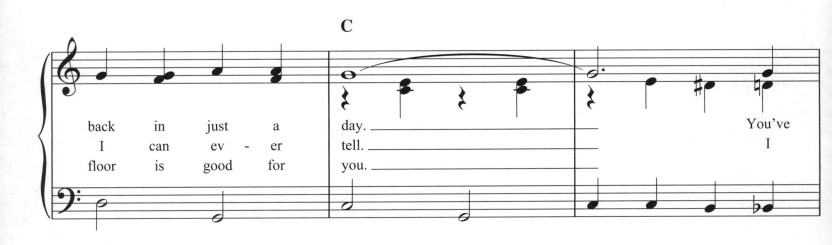

back in just a
I can ev - er
floor is good for

day.
tell.
you.

You've
I

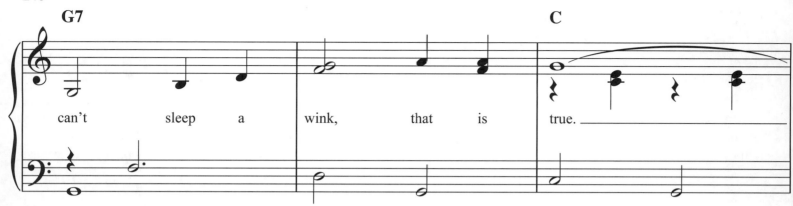

can't   sleep   a   wink,   that   is   true. _____

_____   I'm   hop - ing   and   I'm   pray - ing   as   my

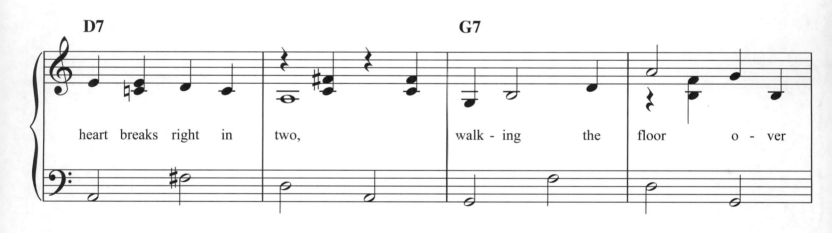

heart   breaks   right   in   two,   walk - ing   the   floor   o - ver

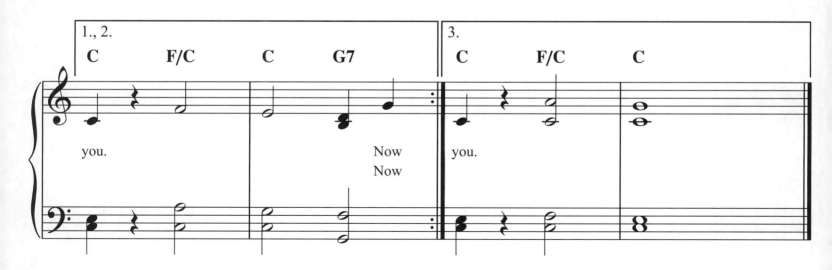

you.   Now   you.
                                            Now

WELCOME TO MY WORLD

Words and Music by RAY WINKLER
and JOHN HATHCOCK

Moderately

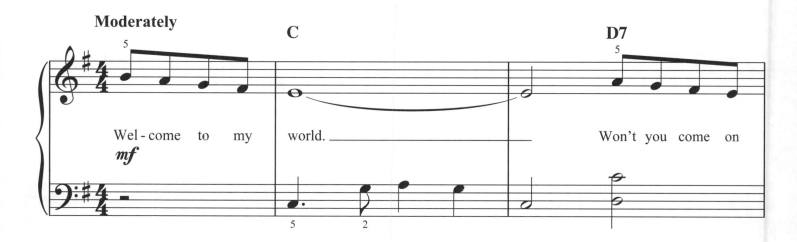

Wel - come to my world. _____ Won't you come on

in? _____ Mir - a - cles, I guess, _____ still hap - pen now and

then. _____ Step in - to my

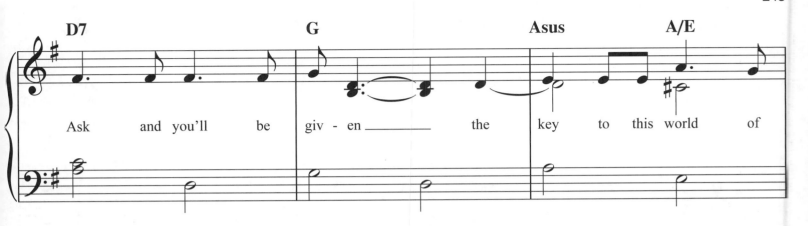

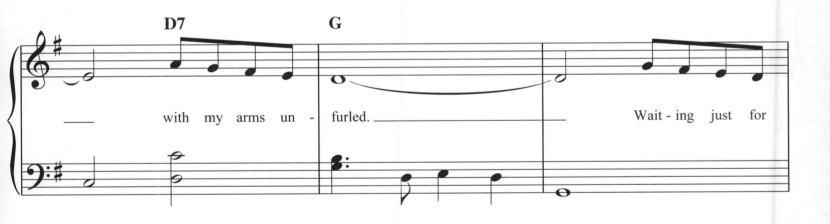

WHEN YOU SAY NOTHING AT ALL

Words and Music by DON SCHLITZ
and PAUL OVERSTREET

Moderately slow

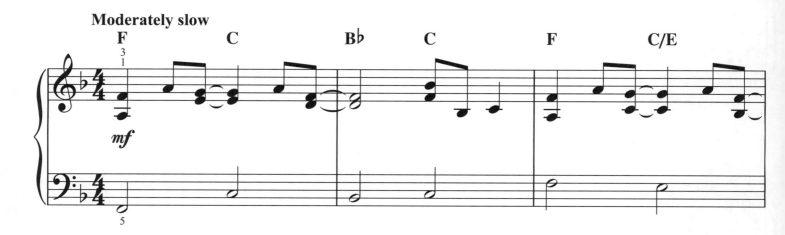

It's a-maz - ing how you can speak right __ to my heart. __
All day long __ I can hear peo - ple talk - ing out loud. __

With-out say - ing a word, __
But when you __ hold me near, __

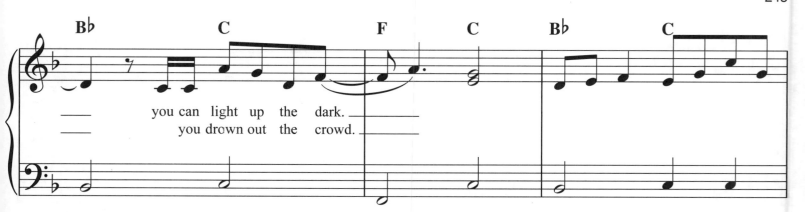

you can light up the dark. ___
you drown out the crowd. ___

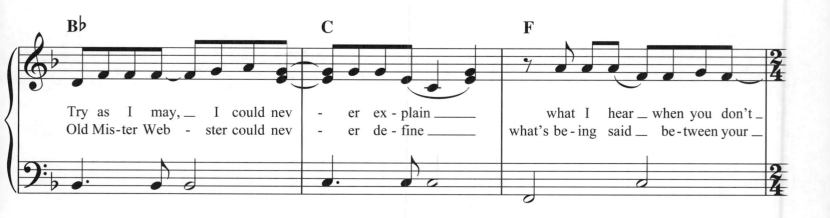

Try as I may, __ I could nev - er ex - plain _____ what I hear __ when you don't __
Old Mis-ter Web - ster could nev - er de - fine _____ what's be-ing said __ be-tween your __

___ say a thing. ___
___ heart and mine. ___

The smile on your face lets me know __

___ that you need __ me. There's a truth in your eyes say - ing you'll __

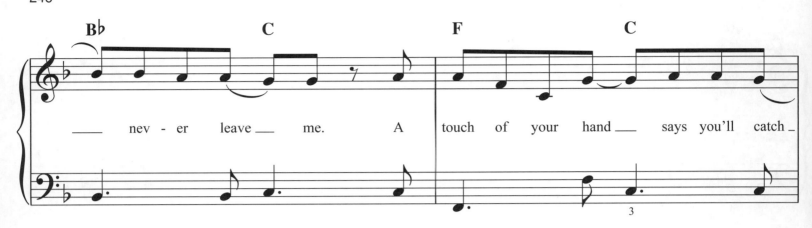

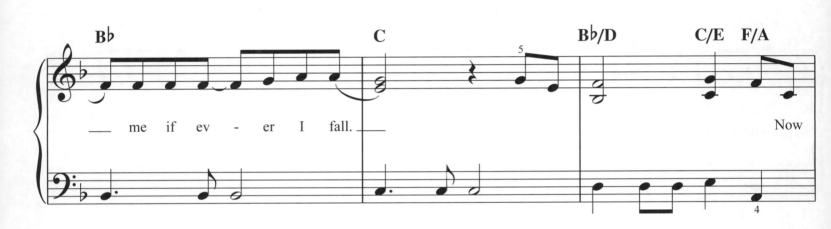

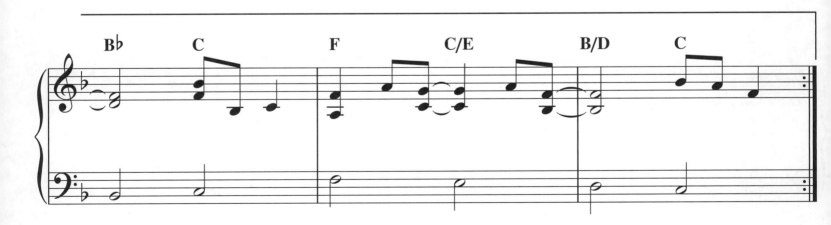

2.

when you say noth - ing at all. ___

D.S. al Coda

The

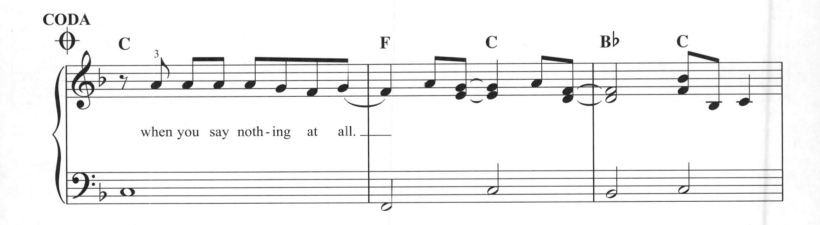

CODA

when you say noth - ing at all. ___

YOU ARE MY SUNSHINE

Words and Music by
JIMMIE DAVIS

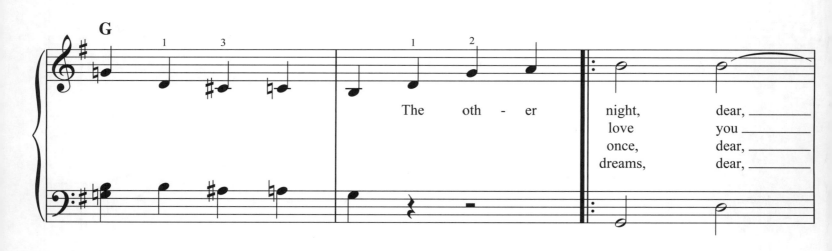

The oth-er night, dear, _____
love you _____
once, dear, _____
dreams, dear, _____

_____ as I lay sleep-ing _____ I dreamed I held you
_____ and make you hap-py _____ if you will on-ly
_____ you real-ly loved me _____ and no one could
_____ you seem to leave me. When I a-wake my

skies are gray. You'll nev - er know, dear,

____ how much I love ____ you. ____ Please don't take my

1.-3. **4.**

sun - shine a - way.

I'll al - ways
You told me
In all my

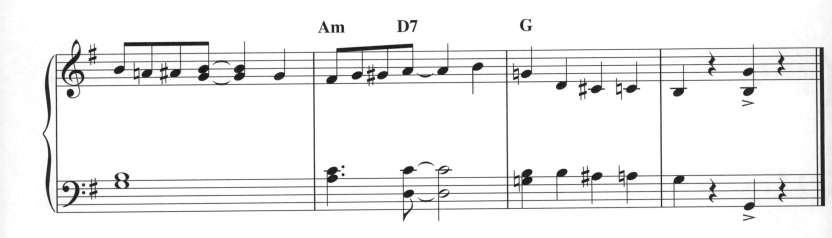

A WHITE SPORT COAT
(And a Pink Carnation)

Words and Music by
MARTY ROBBINS

Relaxed, with a lilt

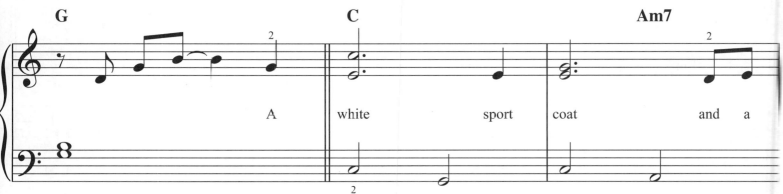

A white sport coat and a

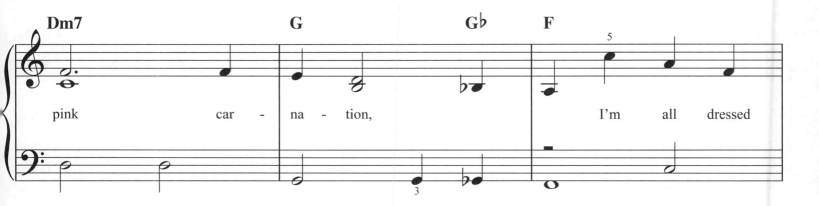

pink car - na - tion, I'm all dressed

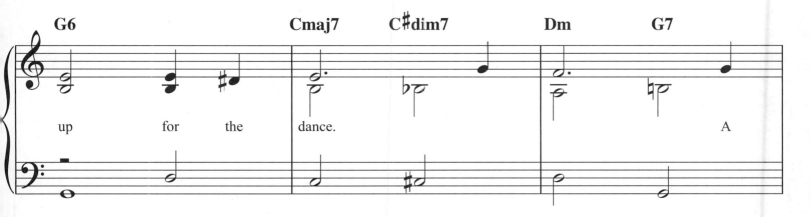

up for the dance. A

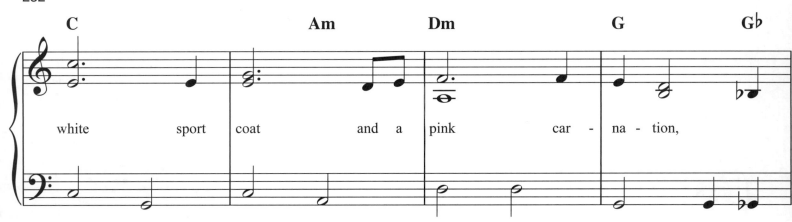

white sport coat and a pink car - na - tion,

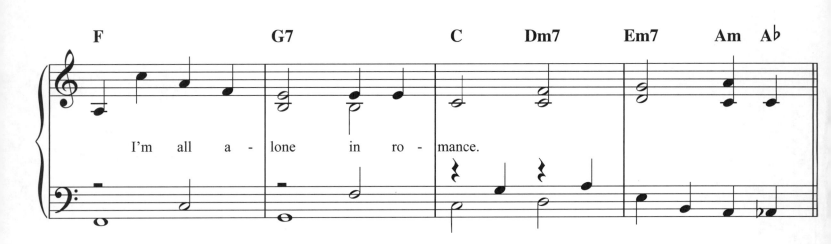

I'm all a - lone in ro - mance.

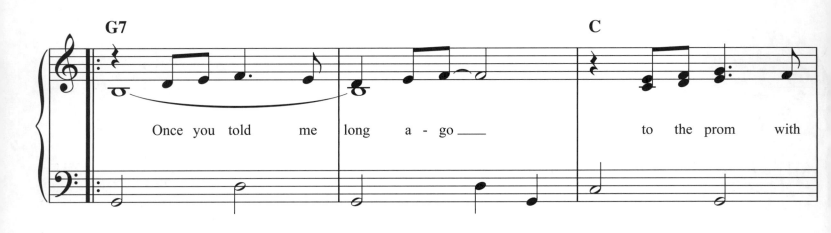

Once you told me long a - go ____ to the prom with

me you'd go. ____ Now you've changed your mind, it seems, _

YOU NEEDED ME

Words and Music by
RANDY GOODRUM

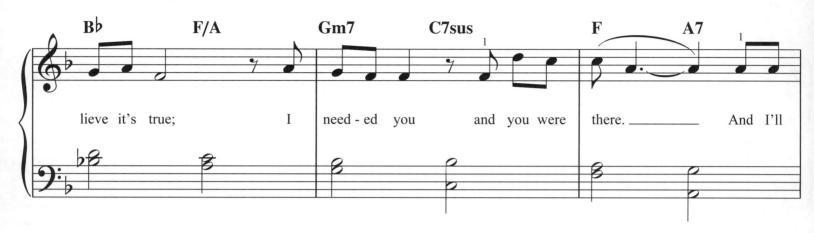

lieve it's true; I need-ed you and you were there. _____ And I'll

nev-er leave. Why should I leave? I'd be a fool, 'cause I've fi-n'lly found some-one who real-ly

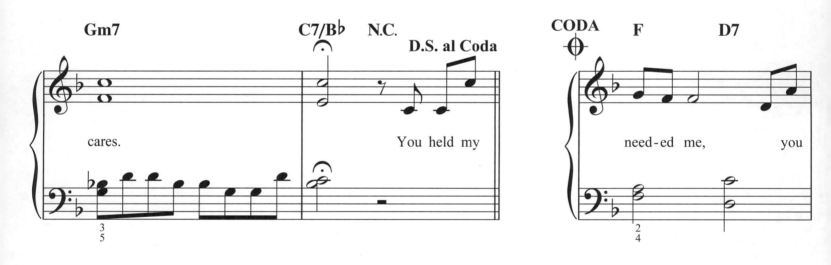

cares. You held my

need-ed me, you

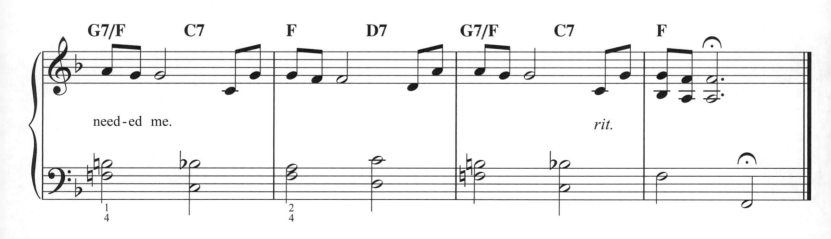

need-ed me.

rit.

YOU LOOK SO GOOD IN LOVE

Words and Music by KERRY CHATER,
RORY BOURKE and GLEN BALLARD

Oh, how you spar - kle and, oh, how you shine; ___ that
He must have sto - len some stars from the sky ___ and

flush on ___ your cheeks is more than the wine. ___ And
gave them ___ to you to wear in your eyes. ___

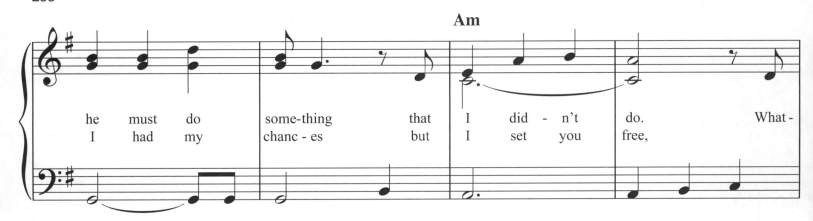

he must do some-thing that I did - n't do. What-
I had my chanc - es but I set you free,

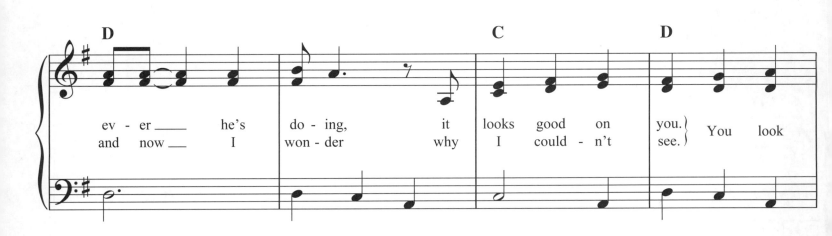

ev - er ____ he's do - ing, it looks good on you. You look
and now ____ I won - der why I could - n't see.

so ____ good ____ in love. You

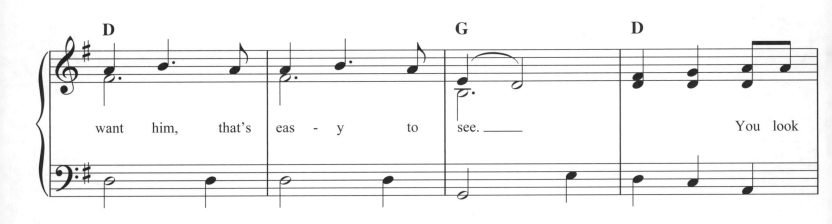

want him, that's eas - y to see. ____ You look

YOUR CHEATIN' HEART

Words and Music by
HANK WILLIAMS

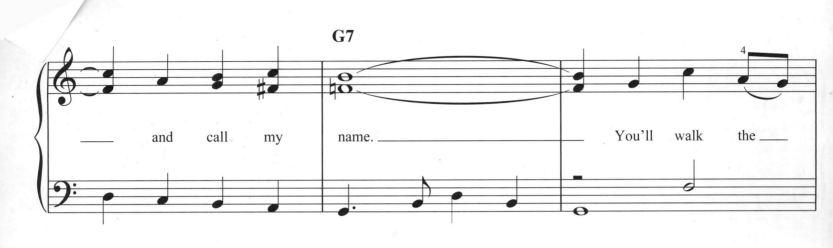

and call my name. You'll walk the

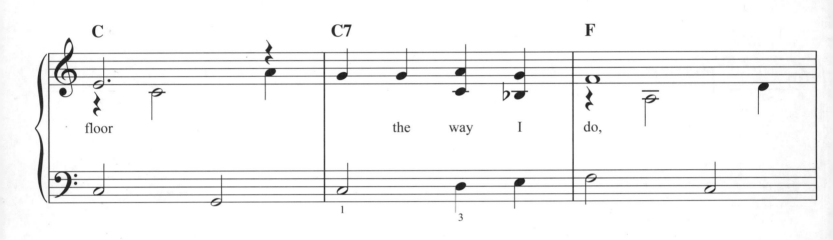

floor the way I do,

your cheat - in' heart will tell on

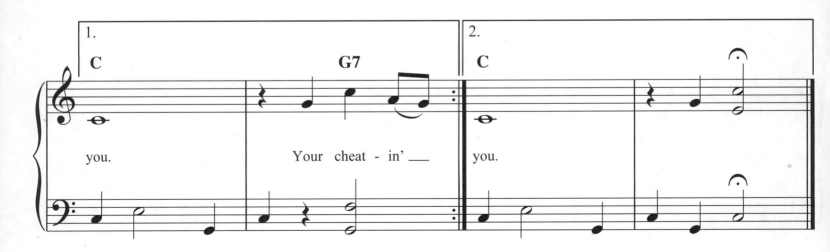

1.
you. Your cheat - in'
2.
you.